DEDICATION

To My Parents

Dr. Henry & Virginia Amen

For teaching me that happiness is found

Along the road known as "life's journey,"

Not at its end.

To the Late, Great, John F. Orofino, L.F.D.

My Dear Friend and Mentor,

For the Inspiration.

ACKNOWLEDGEMENT

I always said, "Someday, I'm gonna write the book" – get it off the proverbial "bucket list." Well my dear friends, finally… someday is NOW.

Over the last three and one-half decades, what I have been witness to in this multi-faceted profession known as funeral directing is beyond words.

I have attempted in this humble tome to elaborate on a mere fraction of instances that have crossed my path over the years. Some of the names have been changed to protect the guilty!

Let's face it - we are all going to die. My quest is to realistically approach the inevitable by adding a little "spin" to the situation at hand.

Many of my client families have remarked that I put the "Fun in Funerals." In actuality, I can't bring back the deceased. What I can do, however, is lighten the burden with a little dose of reality peppered with humor by bringing some awareness that those bereaved do have a continuing future ahead of them.

I am eternally indebted to my editors, Marianne Spagna, Dr. Richard Spagna, and Virginia Guido for their unyielding support and dedication to this project. Their input, suggestions, and time have been invaluable and deeply appreciated by this author.

So sit back, get comfortable, and enjoy the read!

INTRODUCTION

Contrary to popular belief, I do not hail from a long lineage of funeral directors. As a matter of fact, I am the only known member of my entire extended family who plunged into this noble profession. Dad's a dentist, Mom's an educator.

Born and bred in Brooklyn, New York, a career in funeral directing would have never crossed my mind while attending elementary and high school. The mere thought of the proposition would have been ridiculous. Guidance counselors were always suggesting an occupation involving the arts or music.

The convoluted course of events that led me to this phase of my life was totally unexpected, yet surprisingly rewarding.

This once in a lifetime opportunity all began in the spring of 1979 upon entering the American Academy McAllister Institute of Funeral Service in midtown Manhattan, immediately following graduation from Brooklyn College. My love for the biological sciences coupled with tutoring a perspective candidate for the national board exam, mandated for ascertaining state mortuary licenses, placed this neophyte among more than one hundred classmates, most predestined to join their family firms after twelve months of curriculum.

I, on the other hand, needed to find the required one year residency position and hope for the best. After canvassing the pavement for several months, I finally attained employment in what I deemed comparable to a "glorified receptionist."

During this time, I took it upon my own initiative to learn the intricacies of the profession, often traveling to various preparation facilities, observing arrangement conferences, attending committal services and assisting the staff in dressing, casketing and cosmetology whenever possible, more often during my off hours.

Seasoned directors would often ask why I would work so diligently, exceeding the scope of my normal duties. Their view of my aspirations to one day operate my own establishment was analogous to hitting the Irish Sweepstakes. Still, my passion and drive ignored their repeated negativities and following a decade long search, the dream was finally realized with the acquisition of Jurek-Park Slope Funeral Home, Inc. in 1989.

For more than a quarter-century, I am truly privileged to have carved a small niche in the death care industry and am forever grateful to the families I have been entrusted to serve.

TABLE OF CONTENTS

PART I:
BLONDS REALLY DO HAVE MORE FUN

CHAPTER ONE

"I WANT YOUR BODY"

Owning a funeral home has its time management challenges, especially if you're a "one woman band!"

Vacations are pretty much out of the question. As my luck would have it, the phone would ring just as my airport limousine would arrive to whisk me off to some Caribbean isle for a little R&R – yeah right!

Albeit short, my limited excursions are relegated to one night every few months in Atlantic City, New Jersey – a two hour drive from the chapel. As one of my esteemed colleagues consented to "cover me" during this 24 hour hiatus, beeper and cell phone are usually left in the hotel room - freeing me of their shackles.

With "ball & chain" eliminated from my unusually casual attire, I can finally relax and become incognito in this wonderful Jersey shore Mecca!

One evening, my partner and I decided to leave our hotel and venture to a celebrated restaurant on the other side of town. Since I'm an unknown in this neck of the woods, I usually dress very "casinoish," as we had intentions of gambling into the wee hours of the morning. Decked out to the nines in black leather, short skirt, and stiletto pumps, we entered the hotel lobby when my other half realized he had forgotten his reading glasses. Rather than accompany him back to our room, I decided to wait for him at the front desk while he retrieved his spectacles.

Within minutes, while minding my own business, not one but two gentlemen approached me asking for my business card. Taking this as a compliment, not an insult, I wanted to have a little fun so I obliged and handed them their request looking each straight in the eye replying, "You do understand that if I'm to have your body, you must be dead!!!"

The look of mortification on both their faces was priceless as they read my card!

CHAPTER TWO

"DON'T LOOK UP"

Recently, due to increasing real estate values in the Brooklyn, New York area, I've noticed many funeral homes, diners, and gas stations selling their properties to condominium developers.

One such firm, rumored to be co-owned by "pinkie-ringed businessmen," reached out to many of us in the vicinity. Their hope was to deplete their inventory of chapel furnishings, equipment, and assorted paraphernalia, as the building was required to be delivered vacant.

I seized this opportunity, after a recent expansion of my downstairs level, to procure chairs, statuary, and an assortment of supplies from the now defunct establishment. Watching me inspect the eleven foot gold draperies, the son of one of the proprietors offered his assistance, erecting a ladder strategically placed upon a casket bier affording me enough height to unhook the jacquard curtains just below the ceiling.

As I made my ascent wearing my usual slightly above the knee black dress, I looked "Johnny Boy" straight in the eye and proclaimed, "I don't care who your father is – you look up, you're a dead man!"

My unsuspecting aide burst out in laughter as I almost lost my footing and nearly toppled off the rung!

To his credit, he kept his head down.

Fuhgeddaboudit!!!

CHAPTER THREE
"YES, I'M FEMALE – SO?"

I hate to admit it but unfortunately, my generation is famous for stereotyping – automatically assuming doctors, attorneys, pharmacists, and yes, funeral directors are of the male gender. Come to think of it, have you ever seen a member of my profession depicted as a woman in any movie, television show, or theatrical production? Chances are, your answer would be in the negative.

By twenty-first century standards, most career opportunities are open to everyone, with the exception of Catholic priests… so far. Occupations, such as airline attendants and nurses, once predominated by ladies are seeing a greater influx of men. Male dominated professional counterparts, such as pilots and M.D.'s, now host an abundance of the feminine persuasion.

This reminds me of an incident back in the early 1990's. A middle-aged gentleman entered my office during a wake service to inquire about making his own pre-arrangement. Thinking I was the firm's receptionist, he asked to speak to the director. When informed that I was the director, he hesitated and said he would prefer to see the manager. Once again, it was his lucky day and I suggested he take a seat. Appearing a little apprehensive, and indicating no disrespect on his part, he felt it more comfortable if he were able to discuss his future intentions with the proprietor.

Thinking to myself that he seemed to be running out of options, I smiled and stated that "I certainly wear many hats here at Turek-Park Slope and as the owner, manager, director, receptionist, secretary, custodian, and "chief cook and bottle washer," I would be happy to accommodate you with any and all of your queries!"

That funeral contract is still in my file cabinet gathering dust to this day and that gentleman pops in every once in a while to let me know that he's still alive and kicking!

CHAPTER FOUR

"AT YOUR SERVICE"

As a member of the "oldest profession in the world," aside from the obvious one, the average day can never be construed a being from nine to five.

While in college, holding down several jobs to make some pin money, I would constantly glance at my watch much like an part-time employee anticipating the seconds to the designated "quitting time." Now I try to see how I can squeeze another hour into my schedule. For years, I have truly mastered the art of putting the proverbial "two pounds into a one pound bag

My closing times are often delayed not by minutes but by hours. Even if I plan on a 10 P.M. departure, most likely I'm driving home by 1 A.M.

On one very hectic Friday, I found myself locking up just before sunrise. The streets were desolate with the exception of a lone young man, noticeably inebriated and spewing profanities like they were going out of style.

Paying him no mind, (I do live in Brooklyn), I approached my car when he suddenly stopped in his tracks, making accusations that I in some way had shown him disrespect.

Holding my key ring which resembled that of a building superintendent's or jail house guard's, sporting at least thirty of those finely honed metal objects that would make a weapon as lethal as an Oriental nunchuck, I continued walking to my ve hicle. Suddenly out of the blue, five of my neighbors surrounded the poor hapless fellow and escorted him down the block.

When they returned, minus the interloper, I thanked them for their watchful eyes and remarked, "If he had accosted me, he would have definitely needed a funeral director!"

CHAPTER FIVE
"DEATH BE NOT PRETTY"

I sometimes have to just sit back and recall some of the comments that I have heard through the years. The line "he looks good" is all too familiar – how good should he look? He's dead!

I happen to be a frustrated artist. The makeup kit is my pallet, the body my canvas. The before and after results can be quite amazing and, yes, many of my cases do look better deceased than when they were breathing!

Oh, and what about the outcry I hear so too often, "That's not my mother," when I know damn well that I didn't move the wrong decedent from the morgue, albeit, they had me second-guessing myself for an instant.

Cosmetology and restoration are my fortes. Transforming the unnatural into the natural, giving a grieving family a final memory of a sleeping, content, and peaceful relative, rather than one of a hospital or nursing home stint, is what I always consider my most important objective.

When comments of appreciation and satisfaction pour in during a first visitation, I know I did well. These accolades further enforce the principle that having closure, no matter how emotionally painful, has to be better than a direct disposition, where the last recollection is usually that of agony and suffering.

Time and time again, I'm asked how I worked my so called "magic." The answer is very simple as I tell my patrons, "I get a lot of practice doing my face every morning!"

That statement always results in a giggle and a smile.

PART II:
"OLD BETSY"

CHAPTER SIX

"MR. YOU'RE IN THE WRONG PLACE"

have had the distinct honor of being a long-standing member and, on several occasions, president of a business organization known as New York State Women, Inc. We support many local charities and conduct a yearly fundraiser at an area catering hall in order to afford the continuation of our philanthropic efforts.

arrived an hour before our gala was to commence in "Old Betsy," my 1978 classic S&S Superior hearse, with over fifteen donated theme baskets slated for the raffle table carefully arranged in back. After unloading, the parking valet arranged for a space right out in front, for which he was handsomely compensated.

The event proceeded wonderfully and by all accounts, we had surpassed our financial expectations. I stopped in the manager's office to express my gratitude for overseeing our affair, when a gentleman appeared at the door asking where the nearest gift shop was located. We directed him to one several blocks away and thought nothing of his anxious demeanor.

Returning to the banquet room to monitor the benefit, the man I had seen earlier appeared bearing a tray beautifully adorned with an array of Godiva chocolates, honey cakes, petit fours and the like, wrapped in lavender cellophane. He had a puzzled look on his face as he inquired where the "sign-in book" was. Upon further questioning, I realized that he had come into our hall, saw the items displayed, and felt he should not come in empty handed. There was only one problem. He was looking for the funeral home down the block, which was similar in appearance to the building we were in!

Embarrassed by his confusion, (after all, there was a hearse sitting outside), he contributed his parcel to our worthy cause, admitting that he had never quite seen such an unusual wake in his life - and guess what, he probably never will!

CHAPTER SEVEN
"NOT MY RIDE"

For the past twenty-five years, I have religiously made annual jaunts to the office of my answering service just before the Christmas holidays with small tokens of my appreciation for the voices who 24/7 represent my interests after business hou[r] I couldn't imagine being constantly "on call," which was commonplace prior to the development of our modern day communications industry. Years ago, funeral homes would always have to have a staff member on premises or the directo[r] would reside on the property itself.

"Latham's Communication Corp." is located in the Canarsie section of Brooklyn in a rather gritty industrial area. Position[ed] directly above an automotive repair shop, the windows are always sealed tightly, preventing any noxious fumes from penetrating their inner sanctum of switchboards, fax machines, and computer equipment.

This one particular evening was different as I headed up the long, narrow staircase through a misty haze emanating from th[e] floor below. After exchanging gifts and enjoying a cup of jet-fueled coffee, I thought it best to make a quick exit wary of inhaling the foggy vapor.

Once downstairs, I noticed the garage door was open spewing white smoke so thick you could cut it with a knife. Fearing the worst, I shouted into the abyss, "You guys OK in there?" All of a sudden, the figures of two big burly African-America[n] males emerged from within. Unexpectedly stunned from the sight of them, I retorted, "You really shouldn't be breathing t[he] stuff in or else you'll be riding with me," pointing to "Old Betsy" strategically parked across their driveway.

Taking one look at the hearse, the whites of their eyeballs widened and both men made an immediate about-face back into the smog.

I think they were more afraid of me than I was of them!!!

CHAPTER EIGHT

"PEDAL TO THE METAL"

Most funeral directors have the luxury of being chauffeured in a hearse, affording them the opportunity to read the morning paper, catch up on clerical work, or even snooze. I do not have such an indulgence since taking the wheel of "Old Betsy" in 1990. This does have its advantages when returning empty. I can run errands at my leisure, stop by the local Costco, or meet friends for an afternoon without having to worry about a driver getting back to his garage.

Long hauls like a trip to Calverton National Cemetery, ninety miles east and, depending upon traffic, roughly two hours door to door, can result in an all day affair. The smaller the cortege behind me, the faster and easier it becomes - unless the "Slow Motion Rider" or a "Sunday Driver" is in front of us.

One morning on such an outing, a lone limousine followed me carrying the family of a World War II Veteran. This was the first time the young driver, Vincent, had been hired by my livery company and our first encounter. A look of anguish shuttered his countenance, as he assumed with me as "lead dog," this was going to be a very long day. Much to his surprise, as the traffic gods were with us, we reached our destination in ninety-one minutes, a record I have yet to break.

Upon returning to the chapel, he complimented me on my driving skills and could not get over the fact that we were back so early in the day. I smiled and commented, "I want to get everyone back for lunch, not dinner!"

We went out for burgers.

CHAPTER NINE
"THE JOKE'S ON YOU, BABY"

I am very blessed to live in a high-rise condo on the Brighton Beach boardwalk overlooking Coney Island, the land of Nathan's Famous hot dogs, amusement parks, and Brooklyn's version of the Eiffel Tower, the Parachute Jump, which is a remnant from the 1939 World's Fair. Known as "Little Odessa," this neighborhood boasts the largest Russian population on the east coast.

One afternoon, while returning from a cemetery, I happened to stop at the local shoe repair, as a double-parked hearse wou be less likely to receive a summons in that extremely busy business district.

After retrieving my parcel, I approached the red traffic signal and promptly stopped. Out of the corner of my eye, I noticed a group of teenagers crossing the intersection and one young man in particular, who with the palm of his hand slammed the hood of "Old Betsy" with a rather loud thud and then proceeded to sprawl himself on the pavement before me.

The obnoxious imp assumed that I was unaware of his sick practical joke so I turned the tables on him by getting out of my car and approaching "the body" in an anxious manner and screaming at the top of my lungs, "If you don't get up now, I per sonally guarantee that you'll be riding in the back of this vehicle!"

He took off like a bat out of hell.

Turning to the gathered crowd of curious onlookers, trying to conjure up what had just transpired, I announced in a stern, commanding tone, "Any Questions?" Hearing none, I returned to my running automobile – the light was in my favor.

CHAPTER TEN
"OLD BETSY ON BOARD"

On the evening before a scheduled funeral to Washington Memorial Park in Suffolk County, New York, I took on a "death call" for one Mamie DeFrancesco, who passed away while visiting relatives in Connecticut. The spry 85-year-old was a firecracker full of zest and widowed just before I took ownership of Jurek-Park Slope in 1989. I was privileged to have tied up any loose ends of her beloved Michael's final needs, as the previous owners couldn't get out of Brooklyn fast enough.

I contacted a local trade service in the Hartford area, arranged for the removal and preparation agreeing to meet their director in the parking lot of the Port Jefferson-Bridgeport ferry.

Opting for the "water route" was a no brainer, as traveling back from the eastern end of Long Island allowed me to simply drive north towards the Sound. The one hour sail was so much more prudent than going around the horn, wasting another half day, excess gas, and best of all, I didn't have to traverse the dreaded I-95.

I caught the 3:15, pulling "Old Betsy" in between two tractor trailers on the ship's lower level. As we disembarked, I made my way topside after paying the thirty dollar fare. I enjoyed a delightful, sunny October afternoon conversing with the passengers who couldn't help but notice there was a hearse on board.

It has always boggled my mind that total strangers have no problem asking the most interesting questions about my profession as if they just saved them for this very occasion. They more often than not start with the line, "This may be stupid of me to ask but …" I always answer, "Nothing is stupid."

Once docked, I had a short fifteen minutes to transfer the deceased, as discretely as possible, ascertain the required documentation, burial permit, and make a U-turn back on board for the journey home.

With that done, I approached the ticket vendor once again this time informing him that there were now two passengers. The honesty of the clerk was quite heartwarming – apparently on sea-faring vessels, the dead are considered cargo and passage was free of charge.

Who knew!!!

PART III:
REMOVALS

CHAPTER ELEVEN
"BABY IT'S COLD INSIDE"

This incident took the icing and the cake!!! New York City was experiencing a cold snap with temperatures in the single digits. The Cavanaugh family, now living in Red Bank, New Jersey, still maintained a brownstone in Park Slope. This was home to their only surviving uncle, Edward, a confirmed bachelor residing on the middle level, having lost his two siblings years before but steadfastly keeping their former lower and upper floor apartments just as the departed had left them.

Uncle Eddie was as frugal as they come and probably had the first dollar bill he ever made. His domicile was reminiscent of the 1920's, as evidenced by the claw foot bathtub which had been overflowing for several days. Oh, and did I forget to mention that he didn't believe in purchasing heating oil because he was raised in a cold water flat?

Due to this unforeseen mishap, his home was transformed into an indoor Niagara Falls. The ice skating rink that had formed in the front yard was treacherous. Frankly, it was hard to fathom that no one noticed this irregularity, as mail was delivered on a daily basis and accumulating in the vestibule, quite visible through the stately wood-framed glass doors architecturally characteristic of entryways in this historical Brooklyn district.

The weekly (now unanswered) phone call prompted an unscheduled visit by his worried nephew John, who found Edward, obviously deceased and by the way, frozen solid, in his dwelling. After a quick emergency delivery from Statewide Fuel Company, the old boiler was fired up as the medical examiner determined that he had suffered a massive heart attack – well no wonder!!!

The date of death was determined via the postmarks on the letters and magazines piled up by the front door. My embalmer had to wait two days for the thawing process before preparing him for visitation!

And yes, the casket was kept open!!!

CHAPTER TWELVE

"I'M RIGHT BEHIND YA"

It's unusual but not unheard of for a family member to accompany me to the place of death and assist in the transportation of the decedent. The customs of certain cultural and religious groups often demand it. Most Americanized individuals do not

On one occasion, I was called upon to do a service for the father of a local cemetery employee. It was to be a direct cremation requiring no wake service. In such cases, professional courtesy fees apply, with the funeral charge greatly discounted and crematory costs waived.

Upon being advised that the decedent was quite heavyset, his son, Jessie, offered to accompany me to avoid the additional stipend of an "extra man," a term used in the funeral industry denoting the procurement of an assistant.

Together, along with his girlfriend, Mary, we set out for the hospital in "Old Betsy." At the admitting office, all necessary affidavits and releases were exchanged. Within minutes, we found ourselves at the facility's morgue. It took all of our strength, including that of several security guard escorts, to place "Dad" on the removal stretcher and secure him in the hearse.

We exited the hospital loading dock area and proceeded to the funeral home. At one point, we found ourselves traveling down a major avenue directly behind an EMS vehicle with sirens blaring. To break the ice, I exclaimed at that very momer we could technically be described as "ambulance chasers!"

Imagine if a malpractice attorney was behind us!

We'd have a New York Trifecta!

Oy Vey!!!

CHAPTER THIRTEEN
"OH, ESMERALDA"

Since meeting the Castro family back in 1981, I have been privileged to provide funeral services for their loved ones and friends time and time again.

When their beloved son-in-law "Strawberry" passed away, I truly personalized his send off by honoring their request that we conduct a "Budweiser toast" prior to leaving for his funeral Mass. Perhaps it was "kismet" when carrying the casket out of the church - a "King of Beers" delivery truck was seen parked directly across the street. This was strictly in a residential neighborhood with no stores in sight. Chalking it up to a "sign" and not coincidence, it was quite heartwarming. These are the instances that people remember when their next loss occurs.

About a year later, "Straw's" widow, Aischa, succumbed to a freak allergic reaction to an over the counter cold medication, at the age of 25. Her distraught parents, Julio and Frances, contacted me and within minutes, I made my way to the home in the Bensonhurst section of Brooklyn.

Upon my arrival, the residence was swarming with police officers, detectives, and medical personnel meticulously surveying the apartment's contents in their efforts to rule out foul play. They had to navigate around half-a-dozen cats, three teacup Yorkies, two macaws, and a few cages containing gerbils and iguanas. The place was a menagerie, yet kept extraordinarily pristine.

Her mother and father were seated in the kitchen having just brewed a pot of coffee when I joined them to await the medical examiner's arrival, which was to be several hours later. During this time, one investigator after another would appear at the doorway to ask a question, request an item on a nearby countertop, or conduct an impromptu interview regarding their daughter's health history.

I thought it odd that no one would actually enter the room and after a while, my curiosity got the best of me. Inquiring why they were keeping their distance, Frances mentioned quite casually that it was because "Esmeralda" was on top of the refrigerator.

Glancing over to the area she had designated, I had the answer to my query. There indeed was "Esmeralda," a South American Black Giant tarantula, perched freely on the appliance!

Remaining steadfast in my chair, I turned and remarked to those in the outer rooms, "Come on guys, why so scared? You're the ones with the service revolvers!!!"

Years later, THREE Budweiser trucks were encountered during Julio's funeral to Calverton – Damn!

CHAPTER FOURTEEN
"NOT FOR SALE...YET"

The borough of Brooklyn consists of dozens of neighborhoods, some more desirable than others. It is not uncommon, in such areas, for property owners to receive unsolicited inquiries regarding the potential sale of their residences. Believe it or not, some realtors actually comprise lists of elderly, sole-home proprietors to get "first dibs" to the prospective estate. This practice could undoubtedly be extremely lucrative, earning millions of dollars in realty sale profits.

By happenstance, I received a "first call" concerning the death of a prominent local widower whose dwelling sat on an extensive four lot parcel in a very exclusive nabe. Such a plot of land could conservatively accommodate several building with multiple condominium units, thanks to new zoning regulations.

Upon my arrival, amidst police vehicles, fire engines, and EMS trucks, I envisioned a red flag announcing to all that circumstances were bleak at this address. After expediting the necessary paperwork, contacting his physician, and securing clearance from the local medical examiner, permission was granted to transport the decedent to my establishment.

With the assistance of a colleague, we carefully maneuvered our way down the winding steps through the front gate to the receiving hearse. Just as I closed its back door, a neighbor brazenly approached me with an expression of condolence. Before I had a chance to thank him, he continued with, "What are they going to do with the house?"

I glared back, raised my voice a tad and articulated very slowly, "He's not cold yet!!!"

Sheesh, some people!

CHAPTER FIFTEEN

"WHERE'S THE BODY?"

made a promise years ago that I would always extend myself to a colleague in need – note I never refer to those in my profession as "competitors." My philosophy is that if you try to bury everyone, you'll only end up joining them sooner than expected!

When a young man, fresh out of school and newly licensed needed an establishment to sign out a funeral, I obliged him until he was able to "hang his shingle" and procure his own registration with the State of New York at another firm. Since my business was grandfathered in, it did not meet the requirements to take on additional entities.

Eternally grateful for my kindness, he would immediately inform me when conducting his own "calls," which were few and far between.

Several months later, while perusing the morgue book at a local hospital, I noticed the previous removal, conducted just hours before my arrival, had my firm's name affixed next to a decedent of whom I had no knowledge. The director's signature was illegible. Extremely flustered, I returned to the admitting office to inquire the name of the person who removed the deceased. I was told that "Jurek-Park Slope did!" "I am Jurek-Park Slope," I replied, "and I didn't move Mr. So and So!"

With that, all hell broke loose. The previous shift was gone for the day so no answers were forthcoming.

After retrieving the remains I had initially come for, it was back to the funeral home to do a little sleuthing. Numerous phone calls were made to no avail when that young man rang the front door bell with intentions of letting me know he got busy earlier that morning.

You!" I exclaimed, pointing my index finger towards his presence, startling the living daylights out of him.

You see, he didn't want to disturb me at 4 A.M. and thought he would stop in with the statistics required for the death certificate, which needed my signature, later on in the day.

immediately called the hospital to explain that the mystery had been solved. They, in turn, had changed their policy and from now to eternity, all funeral homes had to provide explicit permission and signed authorizations from the next of kin before each transference.

hailed this new rule "The Jurek-Park Slope Clause!!!"

CHAPTER SIXTEEN

"ALWAYS USE A SEAT BELT"

The majority of my firm's "death calls" occur in either hospitals or nursing home environments. Every once in a while, however, the occasional "house call" does come in. When this happens, one is not afforded the luxury of time. Whatever you're doing is now put on hold and immediate action is required no matter what the hour or circumstance.

I recall one Saturday afternoon when such an event demanding my prompt attention was at hand. Mr. Jozef Wiatrowski had passed away after an extended illness in the bedroom of his third floor apartment. There was a slight problem, albeit n insurmountable. One of the pall bearers had borrowed the hearse to move a fifty gallon fish tank. This was before most o us carried cell phones and I was fortunate enough to have his home number. Time was of the essence and Frenchy, in my humble opinion, couldn't get back fast enough.

After transferring the aquarium into Chapel "B" for safe keeping, we loaded the house stretcher and off we drove to the family residence, less than a mile away. The police greeted me in the vestibule and escorted us up the two flights to # 3A. After greeting some relatives and exchanging information with the officers regarding the decedent's doctor and availability of a signed death certificate within a reasonable amount of time, Frenchy and I made our way to the bedroom.

The widow, being of Polish extraction, did not speak a word of English and although I asked that she remain in another room, I guess she felt it was her right to be with her spouse as we removed him from the bed. Once on the cot, I secured t remains tightly with the attached straps when out of the blue, my cohort quoted a line from an old 1970's Department of Motor Vehicles TV commercial, "Buckle up for Safety!"

I couldn't tell you how thankful I was that the widow had no clue as to what had just been uttered by my brain dead accomplice. Looking down, since eye contact with my "extra man" would have been lethal, we navigated the two-story descent with the widow ever so dutifully behind us, watching our every move.

I don't know how I was able to keep my composure as we placed the deceased in the back of "Old Betsy," which to me seemed like an eternity. Acknowledging the widow with what little language skills I had of her native tongue, I proceeded to enter the passenger side of the vehicle, closing the door to an uncontrollable urge to burst out laughing at the stupidity o all!

As we rolled down the block, I buckled up --- for safety!!!

CHAPTER SEVENTEEN

"YOU GOT THE WRONG BED"

Late one Saturday evening, a local nursing home phoned requesting the removal of a longtime resident whose pre-arrangement had been secured years before.

The timing was perfect, because my dear friend, Pluto, had stopped by to say "hello" during the customary straightening up period after a wake service.

The facility in question was notorious for its staff offering absolutely no assistance whatsoever to funeral service personnel. In addition, their off-street narrow ramp and steps made navigation of a one man stretcher extremely difficult.

Within minutes, "Old Betsy," Pluto, and I were en route to retrieve our charge. My traveling partner was no stranger to this endeavor, since several members of his family were also in the profession.

We arrived at our destination close to midnight, just as the "graveyard shift" (you should pardon the pun) was settling in. As expected, they nonchalantly informed us of the decedent's location and we proceeded to the proper floor to make our collection.

Upon entering the darkened room and after confirming the patient's name on the placard next to the door, Pluto approached the first bed as I prepared the litter.

Thank God for my peripheral vision, as just seconds prior to my companion's efforts to move the remains, I exclaimed, "Pluto, No!!!" (You see, that elderly gentleman was sleeping and still obviously breathing!)

Whew…to think if he had been awakened, I could have had two funerals that night!!!

CHAPTER EIGHTEEN

"LATE NIGHT OUT"

When your cell phone vibrates during a weekend late night movie screening, it's usually an indication that business is at hand.

It was my friend, Eugene, recently visiting from the west coast to assist family members during his father's illness. His da— Fred, had just passed at the local Veterans Hospital.

I had known Fred and his wife of more than fifty years, Genevieve, for some time. Not only were they dear friends and fellow parishioners - the deceased was a gifted artisan and handyman, often employed for various projects in my 19th centu— building, which I had already owned for two decades.

This was personal. I immediately left the theater to procure the hearse and arrived at the medical facility slightly after 2 A.M. Within thirty minutes, while driving back to the preparation area, I decided to call the family, fully aware that the grieving relatives were probably still awake.

As Genevieve's son handed the receiver to his distraught mother, it was my intention to ease the anxiety by telling her that her beloved spouse would not be spending the evening in the morgue. "Jenny," I declared, "Just wanted to inform you that your husband's been spotted in a big silver Cadillac with a mini-skirted, long-haired blond!"

Having broken the ice with this news, the very relieved widow gave a chuckle, thanked me whole-heartedly, and finally got some well-deserved sleep.

One hour later, I did the same.

CHAPTER NINETEEN

"WHICH ONE?"

Four A.M. It was dark, cold, and isolated one February morning when I arrived at a major medical center in the heart of Manhattan. Obviously exhausted, only having acquired a few hours of sleep, it was imperative that my personal service was needed after promising the family that their beloved mother would not be taken to the hospital's morgue.

This was before the E.D.R.S. (Electronic Death Registration System) was enacted in New York City and paper certificates were issued by the admitting office to be prepared manually – no longer necessary thanks to 21st century computer technology.

Once all documentation was in order, custodial release in hand, I was directed by security to the ICU area on an upper floor to receive the remains. As the elevator doors opened, I noticed behind the main nursing station, a vast space containing at least forty beds complete with attached equipment for sustaining life.

After announcing my intentions, the lone-seated RN merely pointed in the general direction without even glancing up to acknowledge me, as if I was interrupting her busy schedule.

The room was eerily quiet in the dim light, beings motionless in their beds, monitors emanating faint sounding beeps from every direction. After numerous attempts to locate the recently departed, I returned to the front desk and demanded she escort me to the deceased patient.

God forgive me – but they all looked dead!

CHAPTER TWENTY
"NOT GUILTY"

In the mid-twentieth century, the average neighborhood funeral home serviced its surrounding community and not much more. To go beyond the boundaries of one's area would be construed as infringing on a competitor's territory.

Fast forward to our present mobile society and all bets are off. Deaths occurring across the country or around the world can be anyone's "first call." More often than not, traveling two or three counties away from one's establishment is more the norm than ever before.

So was the case of Mrs. Natalie Ramondi, who spent the last decade of her ninety-seven years in a Suffolk County nursing home within close proximity to her youngest daughter. The pre-arrangement that had been in my file cabinet was so old its cobwebs had to be dusted off!

I arrived at the Sunrise Care Center on Long Island in mid-afternoon. After completing some paperwork, I was given a death certificate, which I filled out, and received custody of the decedent. Before we returned to Brooklyn, a visit to the town registrar to file the transcript and obtain the burial permit was required.

Driving back via the expressway in rush hour traffic was not in the plan. Traveling west in sun glare, which reflected against the white HOV signs posted in the left lane added to my dilemma, as the red lights of a police cruiser appeared in my rear view mirror. Moving into the center lane to give him access, I realized that it was I, a hearse of all things, being pulled over.

Lowering my window as he approached, listening to him request the usual license, registration, and insurance card, I politely asked, "What is the problem?" "HOV lane" was his response. "Wait, I said, I have two passengers." The officer replied, "Your charge is not a person." "Tell that to her children," I snapped.

A month later, beside my legal counsel in a Nassau County traffic court, the presiding judge took one look at my last name and the circumstances of the case and literally threw the book at the officer for his unconscionable stupidity! The judge's last words as he dismissed my case were, "Amen to that!" as the crowded rotunda gave me a standing ovation!

CHAPTER TWENTY-ONE

"THE DEPARTED HAVE ARRIVED"

find myself more and more at the airport these days – problem is I'm not the one going anywhere! I haven't seen the inside of a passenger terminal since 1989, the year I purchased Jurek-Park Slope. Operating a funeral home all on my own has its disadvantages, yet, there is a motive to my madness. I do live at the beach. After all, something's got to give!

For all international flights, I trek out to JFK, a forty-five minute run via the Belt Parkway - that is if the traffic gods are kind. Newark Liberty, in Elizabeth, New Jersey, is out of the question due to distance and the thirty dollar toll to get there. For domestic flights, I always request LaGuardia for arrivals and departures – twenty minutes door to door. On a decent night I am literally back in an hour.

Two major carriers are based here in what is referred to as the East Elmhurst section of Queens, New York. One offers a state of the art remote controlled conveyer belt system that easily glides the air tray, a wood and cardboard enclosure commonly used to protect caskets during transport, into a strategically positioned hearse or vice versa. The other is housed in a much older building and provides an antiquated, winding ramp situated in a far corner directly in front of a taxi stand. Obviously, I prefer the former venue.

I'll never forget my very first pick up here. After maneuvering around all those cabs, squeezing by a station wagon parked in front of their office, I gingerly backed "Old Betsy" up the steep, twisted incline to the sound of raucous shouting and cursing. Apparently, the station wagon I had just passed was here for the same purpose. Ranting and raving, its driver slammed his hand on my back door threatening damage if I went ahead of him.

With that, I switched gears into park, flung open the door and the next thing my agitated colleague witnessed were my long legs, clad in stiletto heels, exiting the vehicle. Initially stunned and ever so remorsefully apologetic, his attitude did a complete 180, offering his assistance as we loaded my charge into the back.

It's during instances such as these that I don't mind being of the feminine persuasion!

CHAPTER TWENTY-TWO

"LOST AND FOUND"

This little anecdote was relayed to me by a colleague and consummate trade man of the ages, Mr. Charles Each. In his heyday, Charlie rolled with the best of them. Married to the profession, day or night, it didn't matter, he worked in the trenches and paid his dues. Today he manages a funeral home in downtown Brooklyn and holds court in the firm's lobby. Inside his massive frame dwells a teddy bear of a man, and he is revered and respected by us all. I am proud to be his acquaintance.

As I recollect, the "death call" came in during the late night hours. A longtime funeral director and dear associate had passed away at his residence. His wife knew whom to phone first, as per the instructions of her late husband.

Charlie had just hired a young resident, still green behind the ears, and together they journeyed through the dark streets to the home where better times were once had. With their two-man stretcher in hand, they climbed the front steps to greet the grieving widow, who thrust open the front door and fell into her friend's arms uncontrollably sobbing, "We lost Eddie, we lost Eddie."

The neophyte behind them, having never experienced an actual house removal, relying on his recent textbook knowledge instead of common sense, affectionately placed his hand on the woman's shoulder in an act of comfort, exclaiming, "Don't worry Ma'am, we'll find him!"

The look on Charlie's face must have been priceless!!!

PART IV:
WAKES

CHAPTER TWENTY-THREE

"THE EULOGY"

Shortly after 9/11, my corporate attorney lost his beloved wife, Vicky. The Messina's have been close friends of my parents dating back to their college days in the 1940's. I immediately drove up to their residence in Connecticut and brought Victoria back to Brooklyn for the wake services.

It was their wish to utilize a funeral home in close proximity to their former dwelling near Flatbush, so I obliged. The younger son, Paul, was a newscaster at a local television station, so he was able to technically orchestrate video showings of various special occasions during his mother's life, such as birthdays, graduations, and the infamous fiftieth anniversary cake bearing the words, "Congratulations Bernie and Flo," mistakenly delivered during their milestone event. Keep in mind this was all new and very state of the art – before our industry discovered the personalization angle.

On the second night, as tradition dictates, the local parish priest stopped by to conduct the customary prayer service. What ensued after his departure was a nonstop marathon of friends and relations speaking, applauding, and eulogizing this one time educator who was revered by all in attendance.

One by one, mourners would step to the front of the chapel to extol her virtues, share enlightening moments and comical stories of a life worth remembering. The audience was at least 200 strong as her husband, Joe, had been a very active member in the legal profession for many decades.

The three children were asked to say a few words towards the end of this impromptu program. Two of them, Cathy and Paul spoke, but when Joe Jr., Esq. was summoned up, he steadfastly remained in his seat and stated that he had nothing to say.

A stunned hush came over the crowd. Quite frankly, you could have heard a pin drop. At this point, I sprang into action by approaching a nearby podium and thanked everyone for attending, their kind words, and concluded with the next day's itinerary. After doing so, I turned to Joe Jr. looking him straight in the eye, professing my deep affection for him throughout our decades-long friendship, but I just had to tell him directly, in front of all those present, "That in all my years, I never met an attorney who had nothing to say!"

The room literally exploded in unexpected laughter within milliseconds. It was so raucous that the staff on duty rushed in to see what all the commotion was about. Joe Sr. bellowed until it hurt. Joe Jr. smiled and all was good!

CHAPTER TWENTY-FOUR
"THANK YOU FOR NOT SMOKING"

Back in the day, cigarettes were considered to be hip and glamorous – movie stars, newscasters, singers, and other noted celebrities would never be caught without one either dangling from their lips or held between their index and middle finger. Even doctors extolled their virtues in television commercials. Areas where this habit may have been inappropriate, such as hospitals, train stations, and funeral homes provided smoking lounges for those who indulged. Everywhere else was considered open territory and legal – even airplanes.

Before the "ban" in New York City, my firm also had a segregated room for such activities. One afternoon just before the customary dinner break, a family seeing that I was diligently occupied with paperwork in my office, took it upon themselves to clean up before departing to a local restaurant for their evening meal.

As I sat at my desk, my olfactory senses kicked in, as a burning odor was in the air. I immediately entered the hallway next to my workspace, assuming that one of my tenants was frying onions in an upstairs apartment. This was not the case, so I opened the adjoining door to the outside entrance. Again, nothing.

Re-entering the lobby area, the sensation was clear that something was amiss. Alas, the plastic trash container next to the water cooler was indeed afire! Without missing a beat, I grabbed said receptacle, to the amazement of the patrons just exiting Chapel "B," ran past them, as my shoulder pushed open the glass front doors and flung my parcel onto the sidewalk, nearly grazing a passerby.

Having realized that they inadvertently placed a non-extinguished cigarette into the garbage pail, the family was extremely apologetic.

I calmly replied, "Folks, we want a burial tomorrow, not a cremation tonight!"

CHAPTER TWENTY-FIVE

"THE FUGITIVE"

After being in business for a number of years, there is a trend to become personally acquainted with certain family members. I buried the mother of one such fellow and several years later, found myself conducting the wake service for his grandmother. It is extremely satisfying to know that my efforts are appreciated when called on professionally time and time again.

Just as visitation hours were winding down and the mourners were leaving, there was a commotion in the lobby area. Volatility is infrequent but not entirely avoidable among large families. It seems that a young lady made a disparaging remark regarding my friend Anthony's late mother, causing him to literally pick her up by the neck, feet dangling and all. As you can imagine, all hell broke loose.

After separating both factions - one inside and one locked out of the premises, where a riot ensued, I sent my friend up the side staircase to the safety of the apartment of my tenants, Curtis and Frank. Meanwhile, police cars littered the avenue and those people sequestered outside were actually being arrested on old warrants! Amid all the confusion, a Cadillac pulls up carrying a half dozen big burly guys wearing gold chains and pinkie rings – I know what you're thinking and those remaining outside my building assumed that also. But … these men were my Gypsy clientele, who just happened to walk in to make arrangements. The timing was perfect!

After our conference, I assured them, of all people, that it was safe to venture outside. My "pseudo enforcers" sped away and I locked up, making my way to a local hospital to remove my next decedent. I returned an hour later and like vultures, Anthony's tormentors were still lurking across the street looking for revenge. Prior to leaving for home, I phoned my tenants to check in and all was well – Anthony was staying the night!

My plan was to conduct the morning ceremonies and once back from the cemetery, place Anthony in an air tray and transport him via hearse to another funeral home owned by a real guy with a pinkie ring! There, he could walk out the front door like a gentleman, with no one the wiser. Alas, my scheme never materialized, as the coast became clear earlier that morning and Anthony slipped out into the darkness after kissing his beloved grandmother one last time.

Later on that day, one of my pall bearers, who monitors police radio calls for a hobby, phoned to see if I was alright. "I heard there was a stabbing at Jurek last night," he said.

I corrected him – "No Joe, you got your wires crossed. It was a strangulation!"

CHAPTER TWENTY-SIX

"ARCHIE BUNKER LIVES AGAIN"

Those of us who were fortunate enough to have survived the 1970's all remember the barrier breaking television sitcom, "A in the Family," the brainchild of producer extraordinaire Norman Lear. Little did I know at the time that "Meathead" and "Polack," terms of distorted endearment that the series main character had for his son-in-law, would be oh so taboo in the Polish community that I have now served for decades. The proverbial Polish joke is also off limits and always redirected to another ethnic denomination, if it must be told at all.

It may be hard to believe but Polak (same pronunciation) happens to be a rather common surname and not considered to be of a derogatory nature within its own context. In the past, I have provided professional services for several families bearing this last name without much fanfare.

My establishment sits squarely between four funeral homes to the left and another four to the right, all along a short three mile expanse on Fourth Avenue. It is sometimes unofficially referred to as "funeral home row" as I often refer to my location as being the "monkey in the middle." Folks are constantly confusing my firm with those owned by my colleagues on either side of me. It is not uncommon for people to walk right in and pay their respects to complete strangers! In many an instance, a knock on my office door inquiring if so and so is "laid out" happens regularly.

Visitation was in progress for the late Jan Polak on one very busy Saturday afternoon. My computer geek and right hand man, George, fondly known as the "Big G," weighing in at 350, was working the floor. He also oversees the daily operation of our parish church and is fluent in the Polish language, which comes in handy when servicing a very ethnic family. Sitting at my desk, I noticed a patron entering the lobby who may have mistakenly thought she was in the right place. Asking "Big G" if Raymond Watkins was in repose, George replied, "No Ma'am, we only have a Polak here."

Having realized what he had just said and what I had just heard was truly comical – you can't possibly make this stuff up!

CHAPTER TWENTY-SEVEN

"I'M STILL BREATHING"

Ever wonder what it would be like to attend your own funeral? It actually happened to Jacob, the father of my friend, Sam. It seems Jacob had lost his brother Harvey, the supposed "black sheep" of the family. Uncle Harvey had been estranged from everyone for years and finding his son, Irving, was no easy task. Cousin Irving was tracked down in Connecticut and dutifully agreed to attend his dad's services in Brooklyn the next day, as his Jewish faith dictated. Under the circumstances, his wake was expected to draw a very small crowd.

Since Sam's parents were both hearing and speech impaired, he took it upon himself to notify the members of their deaf mute community organization (500 strong) not to expect them at the next evening's meeting, since they would be sitting shivah, the traditional seven day mourning period.

Obviously something got misconstrued within their communication because the next morning, hundreds turned out at the funeral home to pay their respects. Since the casket is customarily closed, the group arranged for a large framed photograph of their beloved friend, Jacob, to be displayed upon an easel.

I cannot possibly describe the mass pandemonium that ensued upon the arrival of Jacob!!! Fainting spells, screams, angina attacks, and the like sent several ambulance crews to attend the shaken mourners.

The whole episode was the talk of the town for weeks on end and, in later years, finally evolved into a hysterically funny family account!

CHAPTER TWENTY-EIGHT
"THE SLEEP OVER"

It was just before Christmas when the "death call" came in. The holidays are a particularly difficult time for mourners. Stanley's family opted to prolong his wake services until after the most revered day of the Christian calendar, so we started the traditional two-day viewing on December 26, 2010, a day that one of the severest snow storms in New York City history had been forecast.

As snow began to accumulate, I suggested to Stan's widow, children, and grandchildren that they call it an early evening. I had already made provisions to spend the night in an apartment on the third level occupied by my building's caretakers.

Heeding my advice, they started to venture out when several co-workers of the deceased's son appeared, having trudged their way from a nearby subway to pay their respects. This, of course, delayed the family's departure by nearly an hour, since asking the visitors to leave would have been rude, yet in hindsight, prudent.

As blizzard conditions worsened, the three vehicle caravan of relatives finally set off slowly for their residence, a mere one mile excursion. In the meantime, I scurried upstairs to relax and watch the chaos unfold on the evening news.

The doorbell rang two hours later – the widow, Donna, and two of her three adult children were back, having abandoned their car on some God-forsaken street, like thousands in the tri-state area had done that night. After making some hot chocolate, passing out the pillows, blankets, PJ's, and slippers, provided by the top floor residents, my unexpected guests each took a couch and retired for what was to be a two-day-stay.

We awoke to a winter wonderland with drifts peaking at heights I haven't seen in decades. Not a soul was out and all activity was paralyzed. After breakfast, some morning news, and phone calls to those lucky to have made it home, we decided to bide our time by playing the card game, Uno. I would venture to say this became a tournament only to break for meals graciously prepared by my tenants. We were obsessed to the point that the slightest disturbance became an annoyance.

As the funeral was obviously delayed, Stanley's widow contemplated canceling the long awaited vacation of her dreams, which had been planned months before – a trip to California's Rose Bowl with one of her daughters. I insisted that she not be impulsive and stay the course. We continued playing cards, keeping score, and making the best of it.

After the funeral luncheon several days later, Donna and Debbie flew to Pasadena and had the time of their lives. As promised, on New Year's Day I watched the festivities on television and was absolutely floored by the parade's sponsor – the 40th Anniversary Edition of Uno!!!

If I hadn't seen it, I wouldn't have believed it!!!

CHAPTER TWENTY-NINE

"HE'S HIGHLY RECOMMENDED"

he parish of Our Lady of Czestochowa was extremely blessed to have the Rev. Stephen Jozwicki serve as its parochial car for many decades. Father Steve was truly a "fixture" at O.L.C., famous for his twenty-nine minute Mass and fteen second Hail Mary, which would commence before the last line of the previous prayer was finished.

henever he was required at an invocation or committal ceremony, his signature-closing sentence of, "And I hope he/she ts in a good word for me," was routinely expected. All "in the know" would glance at each other and literally lip sync in ison as the good parson heralded his popular final petition.

 know him was to love him, best described as amiable, charismatic, and unconventional. He was a true "priest's priest," mmanding an "Old School" philosophy. Oh, and by the way, he was a dead ringer for the late actor, Orson Welles.

efore the popularity of "Vanity Funerals" (more prevalent outside the New York City area), I handled the service for a tired musician. The deceased had been an oboist during the 1940's and worked the Catskill "Borscht Belt" circuit. His mily, quite appropriately, hired a three-piece band to play during the visitation.

ather "S" was summoned to do the customary religious rites. I usually escort the celebrant into the chapel so on this rticular occasion, I grabbed the ensemble's microphone and in Ed McMahon style announced, "Ladies and Gentlemen, lease welcome our very own officiate for this evening, Father Steeeeeve!" who then pranced in, analogous to a comedian 3out to do a stand-up routine and loving every minute of it!

 2003, our beloved rector suddenly succumbed to injuries sustained in an automobile accident. He had been scheduled to reside at his dear friend Ryszard's funeral ceremony later on in the week. I learned the news just minutes before the family as to arrive for the first wake session. They had requested Father's involvement.

/hen everyone was settled in, it was now my obligation to break the sad news as delicately as possible. So in Father's true shion, I informed them that their beloved loved one was at that very moment "putting a good word in for our devoted lergyman."

CHAPTER THIRTY

"TRIP INTERRUPTED"

It was an overcast threatening Sunday afternoon in late August. Since the weather was not conducive for enjoying the bea
I left my condo to catch up on some neglected paperwork at the office.

Not long after my arrival, a dear friend stopped in to surprise me. Walter had been riding his motorcycle, saw my car park
outside, and decided to come in for a quick visit. His bike had been misfiring so I offered the use of my toolbox enabling
him to do a temporary repair under the awning.

As the skies opened, we both thought it prudent that his mechanic should tackle the problem at a later date. The decision
was made to wheel his ride into Chapel "B" since this was before renovations added a garage onto my property. After
going out for lunch, I promised to give him a lift home.

Before leaving, I noticed my staff had not yet removed the name on the announcement board in the lobby's vestibule from
the previous funeral. I decided to delete our last "resident," placing each white plastic letter into its proper compartment
within the alphabetized box. In doing so, I took the liberty of arranging some of them to spell HARLEY DAVIDSON and
affixed the placard back on the wall.

The next morning, my secretary noticed the recent addition as she entered the building. Wondering where the arrangemen
were, she phoned me at home. I directed her to enter the large room and waited for her response with bated breath.

After a few seconds, she finally got it when I heard her comment, "You're kidding me, right?!!!"

PART V: FUNERALS

CHAPTER THIRTY-ONE
"LATE FOR YOUR OWN FUNERAL"

The mornings of funerals are often very hectic. Relying on one's time management skills is imperative in order to avoid late arrivals, backups, or overtime charges. Each family service is unique and the duration of the "final leave" is dependent upon many intrinsic and extrinsic factors. For some, a few minutes will do, for others, if you give them one hour, they want two. As directors, we are well aware of the old adage, "Expect the unexpected." Inconsolable wailing, fainting, or even angina attacks are not uncommon occurrences.

I normally save the last viewing for the immediate relatives, giving them a few moments of privacy before escorting them out of the chapel. I request that a witness stay behind while the casket is closed since peace of mind is an invaluable concept.

Running a little behind schedule, I did not want to rush this one particular family. However, they seemed to have no concept of the logistics involved with coordinating their beloved husband and father's service. Having just celebrated their 60th wedding anniversary, it was understandable that Jack's wife was having some difficulty while surrounded by their children, grandchildren, and great-grandchildren.

As I approached the family, I placed my hand on the widow's shoulder and asked her to recollect the day of their marriage. Connie perked up immediately noting that it was hot as hell that sunny August afternoon and the limousine overheated on the way to church making them almost one hour late. Jack however, dutifully and patiently waited for his bride to arrive and the rest was history - highly esteemed by all.

With that I commented, "So he was early for church then, let's not make him late for church now!"

That totally ad-libbed little quip got everyone smiling as Connie herded them out to the waiting limos, which had no intention of overheating that day!

CHAPTER THIRTY-TWO

"DON'T PLAY IT AGAIN SAM"

Sometimes you just have to, "go with the flow." Such was the case of a funeral that I had pre-arranged with an elderly Polish woman, well into her nineties and living alone, with all her faculties intact.

Stefania had arranged every detail of her final wishes to perfection, or so I thought. I remember her intuitively questioning every aspect of her service, from the color of the casket to the floral pieces.

She would be interred next to her late husband, Teddy, at the military cemetery in Pinelawn, New York. Clothing, rosary beads, and her hand-held Bible were all entrusted to my care for safekeeping long before she took her last breath.

We held her wake for just one hour, since she explained that all her contemporaries had predeceased her, before the scheduled funeral Mass at Our Lady of Czestochowa Roman Catholic Church, which majestically stands just around the corner from the funeral home. As Polish tradition dictates, the casket was carried by the six pall bearers to church, not driven by the hearse.

As we proceeded up the aisle, I thought I was part of a Bela Lugosi movie as the hauntingly disconcerting sound of Chopin's "Funeral March" began to emanate from the organ above us. Apparently Stefania had arranged this very somber etude with the pastor and neglected to mention it to me. The porters were obviously beside themselves, never expecting to hear what can only be described as a macabre practical joke. I was looking for Allen Funt of "Candid Camera" fame to pop up by the baptismal font!

As we made our way toward the sanctuary, I instructed the men to look down and keep walking. Once at the altar, we genuflected and proceeded to exit the church from the two side aisles.

I could not help but wonder if anyone attending that Mass heard the howls of laughter as we closed the massive wooden doors behind us! After composing myself, I ran up to the choir loft to ask the organist if there would be any more surprises.

I don't think we could have "held it together" if the recessional hymn was, "When the Saints Go Marching In!"

CHAPTER THIRTY-THREE
"HOLY SMOKES"

It was one of those days. A family emergency prevented the arrival of my sixth pallbearer literally minutes before a church service. The deceased was quite heavyset, so a "five man carry" was out of the question.

Thinking on my feet, I ran across the street and grabbed my friend Howard, a local real estate agent, who always donned a black business suit. Being of Jewish persuasion, I quickly instructed him in the art of genuflection and making the sign of the cross. Time was of the essence, he'd have to wing it.

None the wiser, we escorted the casket up the aisle effortlessly and went to the nearest deli for some breakfast, while the Mass was in session.

Upon our return, my new "rookie," who had never been inside a Catholic church in his 47 years, noticed several cupped-out marble receptacles containing water at each entryway. Assuming they were ash trays, he lit up his Marlboro without hesitation. Before his first flick, however, his actions were thwarted by the rest of us, explaining the religious concept of Holy Water. Howard was horrified and embarrassed.

Several months later, I found myself at his home attending a family function. Making my way into his kitchen, I grabbed a mug to make myself some coffee. No sooner had I taken the first sip, a voice behind me exclaimed, "You can't use that cup, it's for Passover." Apparently milk (a dairy product) was not permitted to be poured into it.

Looking at him with a grin, I said, "Now we're even for the Holy Water!!!"

Chapter Thirty-Four

"And Away We Go!"

Brooklyn, New York is known for its varied, multifaceted cultures. Funeral establishments usually are identified by either their ethnicity or area locations. My firm, Jurek-Park Slope combined both these principles.

Its founder, John F. Jurek, forged his way into the funeral profession in the early 1920's and to this day, the majority of my clientele is of Polish extraction. Several times per year I find myself escorting a family to Our Lady of Czestochowa Cemetery in Doylestown, Pennsylvania, the next best thing to flying back to the motherland in Europe. Ninety miles and two hours later, places us at the shrine and adjoining compound that resembles the Air Force Academy in Denver, Colorado. A small cemetery abuts the massive acreage and although quite a distance away, many return during the summer months to attend the numerous galas, festivals, and pilgrimages held there.

More often than not, families generally hire a fifty-two passenger coach bus to transport them, as limousines would be economically unfeasible. After Mass, coffee and breakfast fare await them on board for the excursion west. Unfortunately, I cannot partake in their A.M. repast since my function is to lead ahead of them in the hearse.

On one extremely cold March morning, minutes before our journey began, the snow started to fall. All of a sudden, there was a tap on my driver's side window. It was Wojciech, the decedent's brother, who quite calmly stated to me that I would not be driving today. I immediately knew his intentions, acknowledged them, and proceeded to call back all six pall bearers from my mobile phone.

Thinking I was experiencing engine trouble, they raced back to my chagrin – "Gentlemen," as I pointed to the contents of the Cadillac, "flowers, casket, bus," directing them to the large monster behind me.

The luggage compartment was then opened and packed securely. As I climbed its steps to my seat, I handed "Old Betsy's" keys to the lesser stunned of the porters – "Drive carefully back to the garage," I cautioned, and off we went.

A half-hour later, my morning meal and conversation was interrupted by my ringing cell phone, which I promptly answered. It was Roman, the owner of the transportation company. Apparently the driver, never having witnessed what had just transpired, alerted his rather agitated employer, who exclaimed it was illegal to use his bus in lieu of the funeral vehicle. Of course I knew this was not true, however his next statement bordered the absurd – "What if there's an accident?" he cried.

My response, "Roman, in that event, I think you should worry about the fifty-two of us up here, not Zofia down below." At that, laughter filled the cabin, our trek continued, and I started a new trend.

By the way, I refunded the hearse charge!

CHAPTER THIRTY-FIVE
"RIGHT OFF THE RACK"

It was a stifling hot July morning as I anxiously waited outside the church for the arrival of a twenty-nine passenger chartered coach that was confirmed the previous evening to escort the Jasinski Family to their burial plot in Long Island. Mass was almost over, yet no bus in sight. Numerous calls to the company's office went unanswered and panic was on the horizon. I fumbled through my pocket phone book until I came across the emergency cell phone number imprinted on their business card and was quite relieved when a live human voice (rather than a recording) responded.

It seems that the owner's wife had gone into premature labor in the wee hours of the morning discombobulating the entire scheduling for the day. As mother and child were doing fine and appropriate congratulatory wishes were exchanged, I proceeded to inquire when to expect our transportation.

Since this was a rather small operation run by family members, a brother-in-law, still at the maternity emergency ward, volunteered to do the honors. Albeit late, he finally arrived within a half hour, dressed in cut off denim shorts, a Black Sabbath tee shirt, exposing a wide array of body art on his upper torso, orange tube socks, and navy blue sneakers, much to the shock of the lobby full of mourners .

Escorting him into my office, I politely smiled and reminded him that we were going to a cemetery, NOT GREAT ADVENTURE!!! I then led him downstairs to the showroom clothing display and handed him a size 48 portly black suit, white shirt, tie, and socks.

Commenting that he was always under the impression that funeral apparel was open in the back, he proceeded to dress as his vehicle was being boarded for the journey to Pinelawn Memorial Park.

I allowed him to wear his sneakers.

Chapter Thirty-Six

"I Am The Hearse"

When a funeral service is arranged and the deposition requested by the next of kin warrants cremation, as the director, I retrieve the ashes from the Green-Wood Cemetery Crematory, located several blocks from my office, within a few days.

What is done with what we refer to in our industry as "cremains," is up to each individual family. The worst case scenario is when no one wants the poor recently departed soul and, with the family's permission, scattering is the method of choice.

Some wish to do this on a more personal basis within the parameters of a privately attended service at a beach, park, vacation spot, or favorite haunt of the deceased. In certain instances, I liken myself to a Catholic priest entrusted to the sanctity of the confessional booth, forever withholding the secret New York landmark venues where loved ones have been eternally dispersed.

Another option is to purchase urns, usually displayed on a fireplace mantle or bookshelf at home. Still others have intentions of "inurning" either in a columbarium niche or gravesite.

When the latter is chosen, I do my best to be present, since I consider this final action to be a courtesy included in my professional fees. More often than not, I meet the relations at a specified time at their chosen resting place. During warmer months, I transport their beloved in my Cadillac convertible roadster, with the top down.

On one sunny day, I drove the open-aired Caddy through the stately gates of Cypress Hills and proceeded to park in the area designated for hearses only, with the filled marble cylinder secured by a seatbelt on the passenger side. The security guard in attendance, not recognizing me, proceeded to direct me to another locale. Pointing to my immediate right, I explained I was here on business. Yet he would not permit me to remain, just steps from the facility's front door.

As I motioned for him to come closer, he noticed that I was indeed bringing a new "resident" in and proceeded to open the driver's side door to expedite my exit from the vehicle. Needless to say, those awaiting our arrival loved it!!!

As of 2014, I alternate automobiles since adding a Maserati Gran Turismo Sport to my automotive collection - after all, life's short!!!

CHAPTER THIRTY-SEVEN
"THE U-TURNS"

When the pastor emeritus of Our Lady of Czestochowa passed away, his funeral service was entrusted to my care. It was Father Joe who welcomed me with open arms when I initially took the reins at Jurek-Park Slope, after all, I did have a few strikes against me being a woman, an outsider, and of Italian, not Polish heritage.

At the helm of O.L.C., he ruled with compassion, warmth, and kindness. The rectory's first floor and basement were relegated for parishioner use unlike other churches, which offer only uninviting antechambers to their visitors. It was not uncommon for clergy and laity to "break bread" in the dining hall or "coffee klatch" in the kitchen.

Before his death, Father convalesced in a Catholic nursing home located one mile from my condo on the Coney Island boardwalk. I would frequently walk down to share some quality time, bring him a homemade meal during the holidays, and attend special occasions with his family. One of the highlights of our friendship was securing special permission to escort him via wheelchair to the 100th anniversary of his beloved parish, surprising all five hundred attendees at the Grand Prospect Hall. To this day, a framed collage of photos reminiscent of that night hangs on my lobby wall.

As per his instructions, Father reposed at my chapel for the customary two-day period. He opted not to have his remains brought to church for the traditional Mass of Transferal the evening before burial – rather, his cousin, Monsignor John would be the main celebrant the next morning with dozens of his fellow clergymen concelebrating.

His niece accompanied me in "Old Betsy" acting as my navigator, since guidance positioning systems were not yet in existence. We were to first pass his childhood residence in Woodhaven, Queens, before making our way to Mount St. Mary in Flushing. Street construction prohibited our entry onto his former block and a split second decision to make a U-turn avoided a potential delay. The two limousines and ten private vehicles behind us followed suit.

Having accomplished this minor hurdle, within minutes, the gates of the cemetery loomed on the opposite side of the avenue which boasted a traffic divider – again, another U-turn.

At last, standing at his final resting place, I noticed the casket was positioned incorrectly. You see, Catholic priests are placed "head first," not "feet first," into the hearse so when taken into church, they face their congregation. The gravediggers did not realize this. I was preoccupied with orchestrating the committal ceremonies and so could not advise them, making the assumption that they knew we were interring a man of the cloth. The norm did not apply in this situation – mea culpa.

I stayed behind and joined the repast a little later that afternoon - after a third and final U-turn transpired!!!

CHAPTER THIRTY-EIGHT
"DON'T FORGET THE BODY"

By now, most of the stories contained within this little tome have been of my personal professional experiences. This one, however, is not of my doing but did actually occur several decades ago before the age of beepers and cell phones.

A well-known funeral establishment located on the upper west side of Manhattan was experiencing a greater than average volume of services one morning. In order to accommodate the eighteen families in an orderly fashion, they utilized what I would refer to as an "assembly line" format.

The dispatcher would methodically line up family limousines with the accuracy of an air traffic controller, while waiting hearses in the rear of the building prepared to receive caskets for burial in designated area cemeteries. This, in my humble opinion, is a monumental feat.

It was customary for the driver and licensed director, permits in hand, to embark as soon as their vehicle was "loaded" and its back door shut by other personnel. Four or five adjacent coaches could easily be readied within the same time frame with flawless precision.

Nevertheless, this one occasion was almost disastrous when the rear door was inadvertently closed by a florist, whose actions facilitated an empty Cadillac leading an unsuspecting cortege to a Long Island cemetery.

Minutes later, having realized the blunder, with no way of contacting the escorts, the dearly departed was whisked away in another hearse, which proceeded to catch up.

I could only imagine the facial expressions, while side-by-side on the parkway, via hand gestures, a turn of the head … and the realization of it all!

Upon arrival at their destination, both chauffeur and staffer exchanged vehicles behind the main office, but alas, the ruse was foiled when an alert relative noticed the change in drapery color that traditionally flanks the windows of the "last ride."

I don't know if a lawsuit ensued, but it could have been "curtains" for the errant florist!

PART VI: CEMETERIES

CHAPTER THIRTY-NINE

"R.I.P.????"

For as long as I can remember, Queens, New York has retained the moniker, "Borough of Cemeteries" – there are actually more deceased residents there than live ones. Calvary Cemetery, located in the Woodside section is by far one of the largest and oldest, established by the trustees of Old St. Patrick's Cathedral in 1848.

Many families of Catholic faith still retain the deed among their personal documents, often producing that so familiar robin's egg blue four inch by six inch booklet which opens up to an old parchment fold bearing the location of their ancestor's final resting place, ever so beautifully scripted by the feather pen and ink well, prevalent to the nineteenth century.

During the course of my illustrious career, I have led many a funeral cortege through its massive gates to conduct traditional committal services. On one occasion, I escorted our Parochial Vicar, Father Steve (previously mentioned in chapter 29), a much endeared parish priest from my church, Our Lady of Czestochowa. Father was quite a jovial chap and a true man of the cloth. It would have been remiss of him to neglect his official duties of accompanying a bereaved family to their burial site for the last rites. Father consistently would hitch a ride with me after his infamous twenty-nine minute funeral Mass and perform a eulogy, with singing and orating that would emulate a seasoned thespian – everyone loved him.

On one particular day, we found ourselves gathered around the flower strewn casket directly beneath the Kosciuszko Bridge, which links the infamous Brooklyn-Queens and Long Island Expressways, one of the most heavily traveled roads in the country. Father's bellowing voice was barely audible midst the constant drone of traffic above us. As always, he finally concluded his prayer with the line, "And may he rest in peace, Amen."

I am known to also speak at these services after the clergy, often sharing stories or adages appropriate to the situation at hand. Since my relationship with this family was extremely close, I knew I could get away with the first words that came to mind – "How in God's name can he rest in peace here???!!!   Who picked out this plot???!!!"

The ice was broken, the somberness dissipated, the group smiled, and to this day, they always remember their loved one's final send off!

P.S. It turned out that this grave was purchased way before the highway was constructed!

CHAPTER FORTY
"YOU GOT A KNIFE?"

Leading a funeral cortege of roughly one hundred vehicles has its challenges. Aside from avoiding red light cameras, scattered among the most serpentine intersections, bottlenecks, and blatant sheer disrespect for the deceased, I've had my moments.

It was a brutally hot summer morning when I found myself in such a predicament at the wheel of "Old Betsy." The steel casket just inches behind me contained the remains of a young man in his early twenties, tragically killed in a motorcycle accident. As expected, the number of mourners present was staggering.

After some cautious maneuvering, I was relieved to have the gates of the Cypress Hills Cemetery in my sights. Upon checking in, we were escorted through its winding roads to the grave site. Automobiles could be seen as far as one-quarter mile away as their passengers made their way on foot to attend the committal ceremonies.

At the family's request, once the minister had concluded his prayers and I gave my usual oration, the lowering device was activated by the grave diggers for all in attendance to witness the actual burial.

Suddenly, one brother made the decision to perform a traditional rite attributed to their culture. Approaching me, he proclaimed, "In my country, we have to mar the coffin, as to assure it will not be used by anyone else." I thought to myself how barbaric conditions must be in their former Caribbean island nation for this to be imaginable. Nonetheless, he proceeded to ask if he could borrow my knife!

Looking at him with a combination of amusement and disbelief, I commented that I do not normally carry such a weapon on my person, however, I could probably accommodate him.

Turning to the crowd behind me, in a rather loud voice, I shouted, "Hey guys, anyone got a knife?"

It would be a fair assumption to say that at least ninety-five percent of the assemblage of men, women, and even children raised their hands and offered to do the honors.

I casually turned to the brother, while gesturing to the multitude, and said, "Go ahead, take your pick!!!"

CHAPTER FORTY-ONE

"SIX PERFECT NUMBERS"

It is not unusual for personal articles to be placed with the deceased prior to final disposition. Bowling balls, cue sticks, golf clubs, and even a Singer sewing machine have accompanied those entrusted to me over the years.

Certain casket manufacturers are now actually mass producing units with "memory drawers" that can open for the eternal storage of your beloved's most personal effects, love letters, memorable photographs, and what I can never figure out, the lighter and pack of Marlboros that led to their sometimes premature demise!

There are several items that I always persuade a family not to relinquish, such as fine jewelry (the living should be the custodians), valued ancestral heirlooms, carbonated beverages (which will eventually explode under certain conditions), and lotto tickets.

In the case of the latter, when Louie, the local bookie passed away, it behooved his relatives to place every conceivable unused scratch off ticket and numbers game in his pockets. During the two-day wake period, I did everything in my power to convince them to let me reproduce them on my copying machine, to no avail. No amount of coaxing could change their minds, as Louie was going down with the real McCoy literally in his hands.

Due to the circumstances, several relations, acting as witnesses, were present during the casket closing prior to the trip to the cemetery. As I spoke at the committal services, I chanced to mention the possible "treasure trove" that was about to be lowered into the good earth and concocted a special prayer to the "gambling gods" to be kind to us all so that we may have this burial today and not a disinterment tomorrow, should there be a winner among the stash!

I guess we will never know.

CHAPTER FORTY-TWO

"THE INVISIBLE DEED"

Most funeral homes practice the courtesy of reciprocity, renting their chapel space to another firm who for whatever reason decides not to utilize their own facility. More often than not, it is the wishes of the client family requiring a larger establishment or a closer location to their domicile.

Such was the case of a Westchester director whom I accommodated for a one-day viewing. As the burial plot was within very close proximity, it was more cost effective to also hire my hearse for the rather short ride to the final resting place.

Upon reaching the cemetery, I waited for the director to finalize his paperwork with the front office, but he returned quite agitated and upset. Apparently, what the family believed to be the original grave receipt was simply a duplicate and not acceptable for the interment which was about to occur. There would be no committal service today.

Figuring that I could be of some assistance, as I knew the staff very well and have a wonderful business and personal relationship with them, I sashayed through the entryway, greeting them with a big smile and presenting my empty hand indicating that indeed, I had the deed!

After insisting that they look at it, as I'm only the hearse driver today, they nodded in agreement that yes, indeed, I did have the deed! Explaining that the gentleman with me had used my firm for a visitation the day before, hence my presence, I suggested that the "check in" continue and returned to "Old Betsy."

Exiting from the main building, my new found friend and colleague looked somewhat dumbfounded as to what he had just witnessed. Asking how in the hell did I pull that off, I shot back, "I got better legs than you!"

Sometimes it's not what you know but who you know!

Chapter Forty-Three

"Don't Bring Me Here"

I am of the firm belief that rules were meant to be broken, or at least bent. Like the bough of a great oak, if there is no flexibility, it probably will break.

This analogy remains the same with the numerous institutions and organizations I deal with on a daily basis. Cemetery regulations can be quite variable. What may be permitted within the confines of one's gates may be prohibited somewhere else, which can lead to unnecessary confusion and heartache.

So is the case with one burial ground in particular, which I care not to mention since the names may implicate those guilty parties! Their main school of thought is a "my way or the highway" attitude and they will not waiver. Compassion for the families they serve is not in their vocabulary and I often say (pardon the pun) "they're digging their own grave." Time and time again, I have witnessed families opting to purchase interment plots elsewhere or even cremate rather than put up with the likes of disconcerting management.

One particular gentleman, who is heir to a massive deeded lot, had a bitter feud with the front desk officials. Their disagreement nearly came to blows, while threats, foul rhetoric, and accusations were flung back and forth. I'm sure that legal action could possibly resolve the matter at hand. However, what this fellow said as he stormed out of the huge steel doors of the main building was truly apropos –

"I'll be planted here over my dead body!!!"

CHAPTER FORTY-FOUR

"TWO FOR THE PRICE OF ONE"

On numerous occasions, family members or even the decedent themselves, via written instructions, request certain meaningful possessions be placed in the casket prior to burial or cremation.

I have always honored these wishes, interring barbells, typewriters, and even televisions (if it's legal and it fits – it's OK), to cremating nonmetal materials such as tennis racquets, guitars, and stuffed animals, which are all combustible.

I do believe and often insist that relatives should be the custodial benefactors of jewelry and other valuables, which could be displayed during visitations and returned thereafter.

One popular item often accompanying the dearly departed into eternity are the ashes of their beloved pets, more recently contained in very decorative tins, provided by their veterinary clinic. Some families prefer placing them in the decedent's arms or atop the pillow or head panel, for all to see. Others request that they be concealed under the casket mattress.

Following one particular cremation, I returned to the cemetery the next day to receive the ashes of a devoted pet owner, whose "cremains" were finally comingled with those of his loving feline companion. George, who has been operating the torts (ovens) for decades, smiled as he handed me the urn and in his thick Polish accent said, "Yesterday, you cremate two!" Thinking to myself there was only one recent service, he proceeded to hand me a small box containing the charred remnants of the tiny metal encasement which had contained the ashes of "Morris." I assumed that it would have merely melted due to the thinness of the metal's gauge.

I stand corrected!!!

CHAPTER FORTY-FIVE
"CAN WE GET A DISCOUNT?"

The majority of my work in the funeral profession caters to those members of the Catholic or Christian faith which brings me most often into a church. Occasionally, I do service other religious venues, which provide for congregants of the Buddhist, Hindu, and Jewish communities.

Such was the case of my girlfriend, Laurie Rubenstein, whose ninety-one year old father had passed away after a short but debilitating illness. I had known David for many years and he often joined his daughter and me at local eateries before "us gals" went out for a night on the town.

The son of Russian immigrants, this WWII Veteran never forgot his humble roots and "Depression Era" upbringing. A successful fashion designer, his life-long frugality gave him a very comfortable retirement lifestyle.

The family Rabbi was immediately contacted along with the military honor guard and arrangements were made to meet at Beth Moses Cemetery the next afternoon.

After retrieving the deceased from North Shore Medical Center in Long Island, I proceeded to an affiliate funeral home that utilizes my license to sign death certificates when their directors are off duty. Their facility is equipped to handle the customary "Mikveh," which is the ritual washing of the decedent since embalming is prohibited for observant Jews.

The 2 o'clock graveside service the following day was conducted to perfection. After a bugler played "Taps" in the distance, the American flag was impeccably folded in triangular form by two active duty US Army personnel and presented to Laurie.

Our officiate spoke for approximately forty-five minutes praising a life well-lived and explaining the final good deed we could all do for the dearly departed known as a "Mitzvah." This action entailed filling the grave with earth using the strategically placed shovels provided by the groundskeepers.

Teary-eyed and clutching "Old Glory," Laurie and I watched as one mourner after another spilled the soil into the final resting place. After all was said and done, the plot was completely covered. To ease my friend's emotional pain, I whispered, "Ya know what Dad would say about this?" She turned to me as I continued, "Go back to the office and just pay half price for the diggers!"

"You ain't lying," she replied, with a chuckle and a smile.

CHAPTER FORTY-SIX

"MUSICAL GRAVES"

We all remember the childhood game of musical chairs. When the room went silent, any seat grabbed would do if it kept you in play.

This was not the case when it came to the Logori family plots. During the arrangement conference for the recently departed Jerry, at least twenty-five relatives were present. Everyone showed great affection for their familial patriarch, from his ex-wife to his sons, daughters, siblings, nieces, nephews, and cousins twice removed. It was imperative that each one be involved in the process by providing information to be placed on the death certificate, selecting the clothing he was to wear, and planning the catering over the next several days.

Although the cemetery deed had been misplaced, his brother Ralph insisted that he would take care of that minor detail by personally going to the executive offices just past the Gothic main gates, where his neighbor happened to work as the burial coordinator. Showing me his green colored visitor's pass, (no longer provided to lot owners after our little episode) which conveniently indicated the section, lot and grave #, I accepted his assistance and would confirm with the Green-Wood staff before the funeral.

Three days later, we found ourselves in section 132 but the wrong site had been prepared. Years before, two separate plots had been purchased by this family on the same day and the sales personnel had erroneously switched the location information which was at that time, typed onto those passes. To think, all this while, Grandma was in #29, not #52, and no one was aware of this snafu, until now.

The officials took full responsibility for this mistake and it was agreed upon that we would adjourn for lunch at the local American Legion hall and come back to resume the committal services at the proper spot later that afternoon.

Two hours and endless beers later, I presided over one of the happiest, "feeling no pain" internments of my entire career!

PART VII:
THE BUSINESS

CHAPTER FORTY-SEVEN

"THE TRANSFER"

Modes of disposition differ from one family to another. While in ground burial may be the only method of choice, others may opt for cremation, or vice versa. One never makes an assumption regarding these matters as either decision may appear insensitive or even out of the question.

When the elderly father of one of my hairdressers passed, I was honored to be entrusted with conducting his final send off. We waked Roxanne's dad, George, for the customary two-day period, followed by a funeral Mass at his longtime neighborhood parish church, concluding at the crematory several miles away.

A few days after the services, Roxanne and her mom, Cecelia, met with me to select an urn, which would eventually sit proudly on the family mantle. A simple cherry wood vertical cube was chosen with the small request that they be present when I transferred the ashes from the customary temporary container supplied by the crematorium.

As I considered this to be a most delicate situation, I suggested we perform this function in the privacy of their home. Upon my arrival, I was escorted into the dining room where an appropriate amount of space had been allotted for me at the table. I carefully extracted the two receptacles in strategic positions, opening both – one empty and the other containing the plastic bag housing their beloved's "cremains."

Both women peered into the latter with awe, having never been exposed to a human body reduced to the size of, what I liken to, a five pound bag of sugar. As I removed the twist tie and circular numbered metal tag accompanying the ashes, I explained in great detail that each case is registered with the cemetery in the event that it can be traced if ever lost, stolen, or misplaced.

As I am a firm believer that "knowledge is power," I continued conversing about the process of cremation as George slowly and ever so carefully spilled into his eternal abode. All of a sudden, a familiar metal object, which was not caught in the pulverization machine, which sifts out any remaining casket material that is fire resistant, appeared in the mix.

I immediately ceased operations, placing the remaining contents down in order to extract the elusive item with my thumb and forefinger exclaiming in my Brooklyn vernacular, "Hey, did ya know Dad has a screw loose???!!!"

What would normally have been a somber, melancholy, and sad occasion erupted into unexpected, uncontrollable laughter that is spoken about to this day. Ahhh – ad-libbing has its advantages!!!

It's a gift to be quick on your feet, even while wearing stiletto heels!

CHAPTER FORTY-EIGHT
"IT'S NOT MY (FAULT)"

As you are well aware, we live in a transient society and many family members no longer reside in the "old neighborhood." Such was the case when relations from Southern California flew in to plan an elderly aunt's service.

As distance precluded a prompt execution of details, we finally met for the arrangement conference in my office several days after Catherine's passing. Her niece and nephew were obviously not prepared for the unexpected demise of their very spry, church going 87-year-old relative.

The anticipation of handling her extensive estate, which included property, stocks, bonds, and other tangible assets, was well beyond the scope of their wildest imaginations.

We dispensed with the normal formalities and just when everyone seemed comfortable and relaxed, the R train, part of the Brooklyn-Manhattan Transit Subway System (BMT) which runs beneath the chapel, rumbled through its tunnels vibrating the building.

After more than 25 years, my staff and I have become oblivious to this phenomenon, however, the out-of-towners were not. Assuming that New York City was experiencing an earthquake, they bolted for the door to seek cover.

Assuring them that all was safe, they returned to the business at hand, albeit quite embarrassed. After partaking in a good shot of brandy…all was well.

Only in New York!!!

CHAPTER FORTY-NINE
"PUT THOSE SCISSORS AWAY"

Whenever possible, I <u>never</u> take short cuts. There are many "tricks of the trade" utilized in the funeral industry, from cutting out pillow innards for proper head positioning to securing side-by-side shoe placement with a proportionately cut wire hanger. Obviously, it's all in the presentation.

One pet peeve of mine is the cutting of clothing during the dressing stage. Granted, this action would definitely make the process much easier and less time consuming. My contention, however, is quite simple – the day I pass over to the other side, there could literally be thousands of very angry souls, who had been entrusted to my care, hanging around bare-assed for all eternity!

With the family's permission, unless the apparel is too small or the decedent is grossly obese, all efforts are made to arrange garments fully intact at my humble establishment. It is imperative that these items be kept separate and labeled.

One of my esteemed colleagues learned a very valuable and costly lesson the hard way. Mistakenly leaving his $2,000.00 Armani suit fresh from the cleaners on a chapel coat rack, his trade embalmer, trusty scissors in hand, dressed the "client" in his employer's garb!

Decked out to kill, the deceased went out in style!!!

CHAPTER FIFTY
"WE LOST THE CRANK"

The so-called "crank" is a tool similar to an Allen wrench, which is used to release or seal the locking mechanisms in "gasketed" caskets. It also functions to raise and lower the mattress of the unit. Varying in several sizes, from four to twelve inches in length, I prefer the latter, which affords additional space between the decedent and the tool's L-shaped handle.

This essential device is a "must have" for all funeral establishments and always utilized during the dressing and casketing process. It is also frequently discarded in various areas when no longer needed and not surprisingly found under sofa cushions or behind floral displays.

Often misplaced by tradesmen and staff members, I'm approached by those searching it out with the inevitable question, "Where's the crank?"

My standard response, referring to my secretary, is "She's in the office!"

CHAPTER FIFTY-ONE

"OMG – SHE'S REALLY DEAD"

As previously mentioned, if I was ever fortunate enough to be in a position to offer assistance to anyone, whether in my profession or not, I would make every effort to comply.

That opportunity presented itself several years ago when a local film maker, Jason Cusato (founder of Park Slope Films), needed a funeral home setting for his screenplay which would eventually evolve into "Apostles of Park Slope."

The storyline follows the tragic loss of a young man's mother and the ensuing love and compassion shown to him by twelve of his closest friends (hence Apostles), and a local Catholic priest in their efforts to guide him back to reality. Believe it or not, it's a comedy that won best picture in that category at the 2010 Manhattan Film Festival. The first half was filmed at my firm. The second half was shot at the landmark eatery Two Toms restaurant, also located in the area.

My lobby and Chapel "A" were literally converted into a studio, where the major scenes were shot. For obvious reasons, these activities occurred between the hours of 10 P.M. and 6 A.M. Throughout their two-week shoot, the crew meticulously restored everything back to normal before the next business day began.

During mid-production, a young actress was called in, quickly changed into costume and mistakenly entered Chapel "B," minimally lit after a wake service. With script in hand, she began to rehearse her lines by the casket, assuming that the "actress" contained within was simply role playing.

I can still hear the blood curdling scream "SHE'S DEAD!" emanating from that room to this day! White as a ghost and noticeably shaken, she emerged through the doorway terrified into the arms of her fellow thespians. "Darlin'," I said, "You do realize that this is an operating funeral home."

The director immediately cast her in his next horror flick!

CHAPTER FIFTY-TWO

"THAT GAY BLADE"

Society has come a long way in the art of tolerance and acceptance of all lifestyles. Back in the 1960's, unwed mothers, adulterous politicians, and homosexuals, among others, were unfortunately disgraced and hidden behind closed doors.

A local funeral establishment had one such dealing with the latter, who turned out to be delinquent in his monthly payment plan for the services rendered to his late father. Martin had more excuses than Carter had pills regarding his lack of honoring the contractual agreement signed several months earlier when his dad passed away.

This aggravated the firm's senior partner, an older gent who had handed the reins to his eldest son. As much as they tried, both men could not see eye to eye on how to handle this situation. Heated discussions became a daily occurrence.

One day, Martin's secret sexual preferences came to the attention of the old man. Seething, he approached his son and demanded that legal action be taken against that "faggot!" Junior, in his usual calm demeanor, attempted to explain to his father that just because their client was "gay" didn't mean he was going to stiff them. The elder man, being from a different generation, did not equate the aforementioned term used to describe Martin's way of life. "Gay" meant something entirely different, hence he shouted back at the top of his lungs,

"I don't care how happy he is, I want to get paid!!!"

Back in the day, before the Federal Trade Commission, itemization sheets, general price lists, and the 1963 book that sparked it all, "The American Way of Death" by Jessica Mitford, the funeral industry was a "free for all." Undertakers, morticians, and embalmers, from what I'm told, were classified somewhere between snake oil salesmen and used car dealers regarding their unscrupulous business practices. The most trusted professions of that era were doctors, lawyers, and clergymen. Boy, have times changed!

Arrangements were either made in the home or in tiny storefront offices, as funeral establishments did not make their appearance until after World War II. Wakes occurred in the deceased's residence, whether a parlor floor brownstone, three-story row house, or basement tenement. The decedent was usually prepared in his or her bed using portable equipment. All required paraphernalia – casket, chairs, crepe, ferns, lighting, etc., were hauled in for the customary three-night minimum repose. What an undertaking, hence the origin of the name.

One piece of information I can share: the cupped-out areas, often seen in older buildings at the top of stairwells, which sometimes may hold a religious statue or vase of silk flowers, are actually casket turns.

Costs varied depending upon the family finances and pricing was adjusted accordingly – nothing was regulated. A retired colleague recalls one such episode during his apprenticeship in the 1940's. In his broken English, a relative inquired the price of a limousine to get his family to the cemetery. At the time $20.00 was the response. "So how do we get back?" he questioned. The answer was immediate...... it would be another $20.00.

And they got away with it!!!

CHAPTER FIFTY-FOUR
"FTC TO THE RESCUE AGAIN"

Here's another true tale from the crypt … sorry … the past. As mentioned, funeral homes had not yet made their way onto the American landscape. If a family in need wished to select a casket, it was customary to utilize a book or visit a local manufacturer's showroom, accompanied by their director, usually equipped with keys for after business hours entry.

It so happened that the cost of these units varied depending on what firm was engaged for the service. One establishment's fees could be drastically different from another's due to individual markups and were changed accordingly with a simple phone call.

One such undertaker, who shall remain nameless, found himself in a bind after an insistent relative demanded to see a particular casket that had previously been purchased just weeks before for another relation. It was late at night and there wasn't a soul to call for a price switch.

Driving them down to see the display in his circa 1939 LaSalle, perspiring profusely, he purposely careened into a city garbage truck sending all passengers to the hospital with minor bumps and bruises, thereby avoiding a potentially embarrassing and unexplainable monetary discrepancy!

Hard to believe!!!

PART VIII:
A DIRECTOR'S LIFE

CHAPTER FIFTY-FIVE
"WHAT VACATION?"

I haven't taken a traditional vacation in over twenty-five years. Prior to the purchase of Jurek-Park Slope, I toured the world, traveling to several European countries, East Africa, and throughout the Caribbean.

Living now at the beach, however, will have to suffice. Residing along the Atlantic Ocean does have its perks. During the warmer months, I return home each evening to a virtual resort, complete with its own swimming pool, gym, and most importantly, valet parking. The breath-taking views from my high-rise perch would rival any five-star hotel. I sport a decent tan during the summer and no one has to know I didn't get it in St. Tropez.

On one occasion, I was asked by a patron, who noticing my bronze-toned skin had assumed I'd just returned from a trip. "What islands have you visited recently?" he inquired. I responded, "Coney, Staten, and Long!"

CHAPTER FIFTY-SIX

"THE BAIL OUT"

Shortly after my divorce, a mutual friend introduced me to a man who would become my next "significant other." Guy was truly one of a kind. After he was born, they broke the mold. Originating from Brooklyn but raised on the North Shore of Long Island, New York, he was half Sephardic and half Sicilian - what a combination! Handsome, intelligent, and personable, he could enter a room and be the center attraction. This attribute sometimes got him into trouble.

One evening, after indulging in a little too much alcohol, he was pulled over by a state trooper, who escorted him to the local precinct for his own safety. This was before DUI's were deemed a serious infraction, thanks to our nationwide media hype.

At 5:30 A.M., the ringing phone on my nightstand awakened me from a peaceful slumber. Only those of us in the profession know what to expect so early in the morning, however, it was not a "death call." To my surprise, a police officer from Nassau County informed me that I had been selected to be the one phone call allotted to an incarcerated individual facing arraignment. Asking who, what, when, and where, the patrolman assured me that bail would probably be minimal.

Having scheduled a direct cremation for that day, I quickly showered, dressed, grabbed some cash, and proceeded to the funeral home to load the hearse for the crematory, located in Elizabeth, New Jersey, arriving at the ungodly hour of 8 A.M. Since there was no time to retrieve my personal vehicle and appear at the municipal building in Mineola, New York by 10 A.M., my hearse would have to do.

As I sat in the courtroom, the gavel came down as bail was set at an amount higher than anticipated. Being unfamiliar with the area, before the age of iPhones, GPS, and instant technology, I contacted an associate who directed me to my nearest bank branch several towns away. Withdrawing what was needed, I raced back to post bond and much to my astonishment learned that my "jailbird" had been carted off to the county corrections facility. Fortunately, I was familiar with that location, as it was adjacent to the medical examiner's office.

Getting back into the hearse for another unexpected excursion, I approached the main gate of the prison, manned by several armed guards. Lowering the driver's side window to state my intentions, he remarked, "Nobody told me a prisoner died today." I gave him a smile and replied, "Officer, he's not dead yet!!!"

You could have heard their laughter miles away!

CHAPTER FIFTY-SEVEN
"THE PRICE IS RIGHT"

Advertising is a necessary business expense. When I took over the firm, I continued the tradition of my predecessors by securing an ad in the local newspapers, usually adjacent to the obituaries. Along with the name, address, phone number, and a few lines detailing my services, I included the phrase, "One day funerals starting from $1,999.00 plus cemetery." This afforded me the luxury of taking on less phone inquiries relating to my charges, which could be quite time consuming.

Within the confines of the same periodical, my sister, who happens to be a dentist, also has a placard under the heading, "Professional Services."

There is a certain amount of prestige that goes along with the term "funeral director." We are often proclaimed upstanding members of the community, church, social groups, fraternal organizations, and numerous charities. This aspect leads us to interact with many individuals.

Through one of our religious functions, I had the opportunity to introduce my sibling to several parishioners, some eventually becoming trusted friends and patients. Jean, the resident comedienne, needed some extensive dental work. After the preliminary consultations, various procedures ensued over a prescribed time frame.

During one of her scheduled visits, Jean thought she'd have some fun by clipping out both my aforementioned funeral home ad and that of my sister proclaiming, "Look, Doc, it's cheaper to die!!!"

What a biting remark!

Chapter Fifty-Eight

"The Travel Agent"

For many years, before their deaths, I would be honored to attend Super Bowl Sunday at the apartment of my dear friends, Richard and Jimmy. Both were extraordinary talented chefs and I looked forward to experimenting with their gastronomic delights whenever possible.

Their humble abode, however, was not conducive to entertaining the forty-plus guests that were sure to arrive at this annual pilgrimage. All three rooms were packed into roughly six hundred square feet of space. Coffee and end tables in the living room had to be relegated to the bedroom to make room for the dozen chairs I would often bring from the funeral home so guests could have seating.

The galley kitchen could accommodate three individuals at a time, since the buffet was set up on the microscopic table, stove, and drain board. Even on the coldest February night, the windows had to be left ajar, affording the guests some natural breeze and fresh air.

After the game ended, dessert and coffee would be served and the latest jokes made the rounds. One after the other would b fired off in rapid succession. It was not uncommon for this to go on for hours, even though the next day was back to work.

I was on a roll one night, rattling off jokes involving airlines, cruise ships, hotels, and various vacation spots. Several attendees I had just met had no clue who I was or what I did for a living. At one point, an elderly gentleman asked if I was somehow involved in the travel industry. As I glanced around the room for some encouragement from those who knew me, decided to come clean and replied, "In a convoluted sort of way, I am a unique travel agent." The inquirer then requested m to explain further, so I indicated, "I only arrange one way excursions!"

Everyone in the know appreciated the candor. When told of my true profession, my questioner roared with laughter!

CHAPTER FIFTY-NINE
"THE ROUND TRIP"

During the summer months, I enjoy entertaining at my condo on the Brighton Beach boardwalk. Whether it's an area concert or Coney Island's infamous Friday night fireworks display, at least twenty guests show up each time I roll out the red carpet.

One evening while preparing one of my culinary specialties, my dear friend, Dave, started conversing with me at the kitchen entrance. As a former commercial airline pilot for the now defunct Eastern Airlines, he currently made his living as an insurance agent, a common ground for us, since I deal with his industry on a daily basis.

Our discussion eventually turned to his previous profession working for the airlines, which I found fascinating. Back in the day, the New York to Florida run was as popular as riding the subway. Flying was considered a privilege and travelers actually dressed in their Sunday best before boarding a plane. I even remarked, "As a child, I had my own "train case" designed specifically for air travel, which is long gone." Women wore their fur stoles and finest apparel, while men consistently sported business attire, complete with suit, tie, and fedora.

While on the subject, he inquired about transporting human remains, as he was always aware that caskets were placed in the cargo hold but did not know the logistics of it. I explained that for domestic flights, we simply book a reservation on the carrier of choice indicating the receiving funeral home's information, place the deceased in the required air tray or combo unit and proceed to the airport cargo area several hours before departure to ensure loading.

At this point, Dave inquired about the fees involved regarding the weight, mileage, etc. I gave him an example based on a recent shipment I had made to Atlanta, Georgia. To my recollection, the fare at the time was approximately $450.00.

As he sipped on his cocktail, he nodded approvingly and asked, "Is that round trip?" I looked at him with a straight face and replied, "I don't want them back!" Realizing what he had just said, we had a good laugh and another drink!

CHAPTER SIXTY

"KILL ME NOW"

My very dear colleague and friend, who we'll call Chuck for the purposes of this narrative is a gambler. He got himself into a jam with the local shylocks. Faust, who sold his soul to the devil, had a better chance for survival, as Chuck's weekly "vig" (interest), yet alone principal, could barely be met.

His "financial ship" was sinking faster than the Titanic when, after leaving the preparation room following an all night embalming marathon, he was involved in a very serious automobile accident.

After being pulled from the wreckage of his recently purchased removal van (now a total loss), he clutched his forearm "v" shaped from a compound fracture, affording him no way to make a living to repay his debt. Uncontrollably lamenting, "I'm dead, I'm dead," he lay on a cold uninviting pavement awaiting the ambulance's arrival. As his words were uttered again and again, a female bystander, who witnessed the collision approached and said, "No sir, you're alive!"

Oblivious to the excruciating pain and subsequent surgeries that would ensue, Chuck blurted back in a delusional stupor "No Ma'am, you don't understand, I am truly dead!" as the approaching sirens drowned out his mental, physical, and verbal anguish!

He has since finalized his debt with those gentlemen thanks to the generosity and compassion of another wonderful and endearing friend who shall remain anonymous!

CHAPTER SIXTY-ONE
"THERE'S A DEAD GUY IN HERE"

Down on his luck and facing a probable divorce, Harry came back to Brooklyn and showed up at the doorstep of his former employer, a local funeral home, where he had apprenticed several years earlier. Feeling sorry for the fellow, the owner allowed him to bunk in the downstairs employee lounge abutting the preparation area. Noisy but warm and clean, Harry took the offer.

Several weeks went by with Harry pinch-hitting whenever he could in appreciation for the humble lodgings, as he attempted to get his life together. One morning as the proprietor arrived for work, he noticed the TV still blaring as Harry slept on the couch. Passing by, he turned down the volume so it would not disturb the mourners when they arrived for services.

Returning after the committal ceremonies, he observed Harry, still on the couch and thought it strange that he was still sleeping. Attempting to arouse him, it was immediately obvious that Harry would not be waking up, as he had died of an apparent massive heart attack - probably during the night.

911 was called, with the first words, "I need the police – there's a dead man here at my funeral home!" A click was heard on the receiving end! A second try produced the same effect! Finally after realizing that this did indeed sound like a prank, the third and final plea for help began with, "This is not a practical joke!!!!!!"

Harry was sent back down to Florida for burial.

Chapter Sixty-Two

"She Moved"

When one is in the funeral profession, many hats are worn. Not only do we attend to the deposition of the deceased, it is those family members left behind who rely on us for assistance with many issues, such as clothing donations, vacating apartments of furniture, and life's simple everyday needs that the decedent might have fulfilled.

Heddy, an elderly lady, was a perfect example of this. Having lost her sister and brother-in-law within an eighteen month period, she was left all alone with no living relatives. After pre-planning her funeral, she requested my help in obtaining approval from a local senior organization to afford her membership for low cost bus transportation.

She was surely a candidate, meeting every requirement necessary for acceptance as a golden-ager. Immediate placement should have been rendered. This however was not the case. Bureaucracy and red tape prolonged her application for well over a year.

During this extended wait period, as expected, my dear friend passed away. All details of her pre-arrangement were executed as to her wishes and she was finally reunited with her husband who had predeceased her by forty years.

Several months later, I received a phone call from a representative of the Elder Ride Corporation. It seems that they could not contact Heddy at her residence, since the phone had been disconnected and no further information was available. I had forgotten that my number had been given as an alternate contact. The woman at the other end apologized for the delay asking if I would be so kind as to relay to Heddy the message that she had been accepted for the aforementioned services.

After gathering my composure, I replied, "She moved but I would be happy to give you her new address." The caller was ready at her computer terminal feeding information I gave her into the address slot on the screen. At that point I stated, "All correspondence should be forwarded to 3620 – Tilden Avenue, Brooklyn, New York 11203." She then inquired if this was a nursing home or assisted living residence for an "in care of" name.

I replied, "Holy Cross Cemetery" and promptly hung up!!!

CHAPTER SIXTY-THREE

"I GOT YOUR MEASUREMENTS"

It was the summer of 1986 when my parents decided to treat me and my then husband to a three-night stay at an Atlantic City casino. One evening, Dad surprised us all when he got front row seats at the Don Rickles show by generously greasing the palm of the theater's maitre d'. Our table actually abutted the stage giving us the possibility of close interaction as "Mr. Warmth" made his grand entrance, ribbing everyone in sight.

I knew we were in trouble when he approached my spouse and invited him up to center stage. "What's your name?" the comedian asked. My other half, who was of Italian descent with an ethnic moniker to match, dutifully answered. The comic's response was, "I had that disease in World War II!"

The next question was the killer when Mr. Rickles inquired, "What do you do for a living?" "Funeral Director" was promptly answered and without missing a beat, the showman's wired microphone dropped to the floor with a rather loud thud.

Being the gentlemen, his "victim" reached down, grabbed the attached cord and used it to measure the absolutely stunned entertainer, who was so taken aback by this unexpected role reversal that he was actually speechless!

Needless to say, the crowd roared. After what seemed like an eternity, the laughter waned to the star's comment "Ok, Guinea - 1, Jew – Zip!"

Later on that evening, our gracious host presented our entourage with a bottle of fine champagne and we were congratulated throughout the night by those in attendance for "zinging" it to the "King of the Zinger!!!"

CHAPTER SIXTY-FOUR

"HE COULDN'T WAIT!"

Most families still uphold the long standing tradition of dining out after the funeral service, usually at a local restaurant, catering hall, or occasionally their residence. I have had the honor and privilege of attending many such repasts over the years, yet one in particular stands out.

A popular neighborhood guy, known as "Viper," passed away unexpectedly leaving his childless middle-aged wife alone and devastated. His friends rallied around her in support during the two-day wake period and I literally pulled out all the stops to make his service as unique and unforgettable as he was.

It has always been my philosophy to accommodate each individual funeral with as much personalization as possible, as long as it is legal. Viper's was no exception. Custom floral arrangements, photographs, videos, and treasured sports paraphernalia were displayed everywhere for the hundreds of mourners to admire causing endless proclamations of one fond memory after another.

Following the committal ceremonies the next morning, all convened back at a local Veterans Post for the buffet luncheon. I usually make my entrance twenty minutes or so behind the guests, as I prefer to return to the chapel to square away any unfinished business before lunch.

Upon walking into the VFW's back hall, I was greeted by a standing ovation and accolades of praise for conducting such a wonderful send off, which prompted one fellow, with a beer in hand to exclaim how they would never consider hiring another funeral firm. A second compadre shouted from the other side of the room, "Yeah, I can't wait to die!" followed by uncontrollable applause and laughter!

I had the baked ziti.

CHAPTER SIXTY-FIVE

"A MATTER OF LIFE OR DEATH???"

Through a close friend, I was introduced to a physician, Dr. Stein, from Bayside, New York. The good doctor's illustrious career began with a residency in emergency room trauma. After more than a decade practicing in this extremely stressful field, a tragic accident case under his care (which gained worldwide notoriety) finally broke the camel's back. This horrific event caused him to seek out another specialty - at the other end of the medical spectrum - obstetrics and gynecology.

The nature of this particular field required all staff to live in close proximity to the affiliated hospital center. Throughout our relationship, during the nights he was on call, I would stay at his place in Queens, since his profession demanded a greater sense of urgency than mine to expediently get to his clientele. I had the luxury of using a trade service or simply taking the "first call" information from the family, scheduling the removal the next day, and returning to bed – he had no choice but to get up and go.

This was during the time when beepers were used by our respective answering services to contact us, rather than cell phones. When that familiar "tone" would interrupt our sleep in the middle of the night, the sound was so generic that initially neither one of us knew if "someone was coming in" or "someone was going out!"

CHAPTER SIXTY-SIX

"SURE HE'S DEAD?"

There's always one in the neighborhood – a disgruntled old geezer whose main function is to be forever mad at the world. So was the case of Murray, a crotchety soul who held court in front of the local grocery store, rain or shine. By design, he had nothing nice to say about anything or anyone.

Constant complaints regarding the weather, politics, news, and life in general were echoed throughout the area on a daily basis. There was no pleasing this man, as evidenced by the many wives that left him in the dust.

Community organizations tolerated his presence at monthly meetings but limited his participation in civic events, knowing full well that he would discover something with which to find fault.

Senior groups cringed when he would show up for weekly bingo marathons or bus trips to Atlantic City. To be blunt, no one liked him due to his demeanor, and rightly so.

Attending a parish dinner dance one evening, I overheard an elderly lay council member comment about a recent funeral service held at my establishment for a revered church congregant. It was standing room only. He then remarked that if it had been for Murray, the place would have been empty.

 I had all I could do not to divulge what I was really thinking.

My chapel would probably be mobbed because everybody would want to make certain he's dead!!!

CHAPTER SIXTY-SEVEN
"DON'T CALL ME IN THE MORNING"

One thing about this crazy business of mine is that it will never be a "nine to five job." If, on any given evening, I should be fortunate enough to get home before midnight, my doorman, Rudy, asks his standard question with a Romanian accent, "Miss, is everything alright?"

Funeral directors are akin to bankers – once the doors lock for the day, they remain behind, tabulating and computing until the last penny is accounted for. I often find the seclusion of my office "sanctuary" so welcoming once the last visitor leaves. The phones are quiet and I can work uninterrupted, having no more insurance claims to process or letters of attendance to type. You'd be surprised how much you can get done at 2 A.M.! As a matter of fact, that is the exact hour I am actually putting these words on paper.

Nonetheless, once I call answering service from my phone, I can return the electronic appendage that never leaves my side into its cradle. That is until my secretary starts taking incoming calls not one minute before 10 A.M. the following morning. Do keep in mind that I do not relish early funerals – if a religious service, such as a Mass is scheduled for 9 A.M., it would not be unusual that I would stop by the rectory asking Father if he's trying to kill me?!

I am known to be a sound sleeper but am attuned to the "ring" as a mother is to her crying infant. An early morning call came in at around 5 A.M. It was not answering service with an expected "death call." Instead it was a wrong number. The gentlemen on the other end sounded inebriated, professing his sorrow to his wife for whatever the hell he must have done just hours before.

After informing him, to no avail, that he had dialed the wrong number, I thought to hang up, yet there was the possibility that he would either call back or wake up another poor soul. I made the decision with nose still nestled in my pillow, to forgive the incredulous idiot by appeasing him and absolving every hedonistic act of cruelty inflicted on whomever, ending with the statement, "Yes darling, you may come home!"

I'd have loved to have been a fly on the wall for that little reunion!

Serves him right for waking me up – ahhhh, revenge is sweet!

Chapter Sixty-Eight

"Too Many Signs"

In all my years as a funeral director, I have seen and heard it all. Yet, I've never discounted the experiences of others regarding the possibility of an afterlife. Many have approached me with intriguing scenarios involving the mysterious scent of Mom's perfume filling a room, the lingering aroma of Grandpa's pipe, the appearance of a morning dove on a windowsill, a tightened faucet inexplicably gushing water, or a motorized appliance suddenly turning itself on.

I usually respond that these so-called "signs" should be taken as a source of comfort that their loved one, who is no longer with us, is OK on the "other side."

Before he passed, my significant other, Guy (previously mentioned in chapter 56), and I often spoke about this phenomenon. He promised that he would do everything in his power to "connect" with me when that fateful time arrived.

Unfortunately, it did in October, 2005, on what would have been his father's eightieth birthday. I'd like to think that Sydney reached down and brought his son home from the condo we shared at the beach…and then it started.

Ladies and Gentlemen – **I AM NOT DELUSIONAL**, but what transpired over the days and weeks following his death was so compelling, if I wasn't privy to it, I might not have believed it.

Framed pictures fell from the walls. Objects on counters toppled to the floor. Misplaced items appeared out of nowhere. During a morphine induced stupor, the "oil painting" that he kept mentioning, turned out to be the recently purchased masterpiece of the proprietor of the funeral home I utilized for his wake service on Long Island. It was prominently displayed above the fireplace in the very room in which he reposed. The priest's eulogy at Mass included a mention of his extensive British sports car collection and at that very moment, the lights began to flicker in the sanctuary. His three sisters and I were spellbound.

Several weeks later, while preparing my balcony furniture for winter storage, I was convinced when a seagull alighted on the railing. This had never happened before or since, as shore birds are normally antisocial. My avian visitor was perched within a few feet from my presence, another anomaly.

Somehow, I knew it was him, as during our nine year relationship, he was aware of my love for the ocean and my favorite sound, that of the gull. Ten minutes passed, (I'm not exaggerating), while I sat and chatted with my feathered friend and finally lamented that he should go – I would be alright and there would be no need for any further "signs." He then spread his wings and I watched, teary-eyed, as he blended into the horizon.

Looking down, I noticed he had left me a "calling card" on the terrace floor. Yep…it was him!!!

I repeat – **I AM NOT DELUSIONAL!!!**

CHAPTER SIXTY-NINE

"DYING FOR A SMOKE"

I have been the subject of several TV documentaries over the years, most recently "Undertaker in Heels" for Germany's ARD television, which aired on their version of our "Sixty Minutes" back in 2012.

The pilot for "Amen to That" never materialized since it was considered more of a reality format, where being scripted was out of the question.

I was however involved in a spoof commercial for the now popular electronic cigarette. Ninety seconds in length, it required no editing and was shorter than most of my eulogies given at graveside services!

It commences with me driving my XLR convertible through what appears to be a tree-canopied country lane. Coming to a stop, I exit the vehicle, look straight into the camera and begin my spiel by saying, "You may remember me from cable TV's "Dearly Departed," and if you smoke, you just might earn that title sooner than later! That's why I'm here to tell you about electronic smoking." I then proceed to announce the toll free number and website of the company and explain the wonderful advantages of the product, its price, the initial starter kit, filter flavors, and nicotine strengths.

Continuing, I say, "They are odor free, toxin free, and you and your clothing will never smell like an ashtray again!" followed by the fact that smoking is prohibited almost everywhere nowadays. I also mention that "when I get home at night, I charge my cell phone and my cigarette!"

The grand finale culminates when I recommend that the viewer should give it a try for after all, "Life's short and I'd much rather be driving around in my little Caddy than taken for a ride in my other one!"

At this point, the camera pans across the aforementioned rural road, exposing "Old Betsy" and the surrounding tombstones, as we are filming in Green-Wood Cemetery! As I pass the hearse's open back door, I slam it shut and remark, "So do it now or else, you just might be seeing me!" I walk out of the visual shot with only the sound of my clicking high heels on the pavement.

The credits then phase in: This testimonial courtesy of Jurek-Park Slope Funeral Home, Inc. and Park Slope Film Productions, Brooklyn, New York!

I have since formed Amen to That Productions, LLC and anticipate many more projects in the future after this first venture,

"I'M DYING TO TELL YA!"

CHAPTER SEVENTY

"A FEW MORE QUIPS"

People are fascinated that my last name happens to be Amen, after all, it does mean "The End!"

How many times through the years have I been told that someone is "Dying to see me?"

Have you ever seen a "Dead End" sign posted on a street abutting a cemetery gate?

I cannot count how many times I have been asked, "How's business?" Do they expect me to say "Dead?"

As a courtesy, Chapel "A" sometimes serves as a makeshift confessional for those wishing to receive Communion at the next morning's funeral Mass. I never partake – Father doesn't have enough time!

Attempting to drum up some business for my dear friend and hairstylist Karolin, the owner of a local beauty salon, we parked "Old Betsy" by several area high schools and handed out flyers which read "Look Drop Dead Gorgeous On Prom Night!"

I often hear the term, "I'm Dying," blurted out when one is either very hot or very tired. This verbal exaggeration is always answered with, "Don't talk shop – I'm off duty right now!"

Rosedale Cemetery in New Jersey boasts a headstone that reads, "I'd rather be at OTB!"

Some folks inquire about "time payments" but never "lay away plans" when making arrangements.

I just can't seem to adjust a gentleman's tie in the vertical position!

I always use a neon lime green sign placed in the back window of "Old Betsy" whenever parked in a friend's driveway which reads "Just Visiting!"

I try to greet families by saying "Morning" at A.M. services, after all, what's good about it?

I find it surreal when approaching the crematory on a direct cremation, listening to WCBS FM while the DJ's selection is none other than "Disco Inferno!"

I sometimes service a family several times in a one year period; ergo, they have me on "speed dial!!!"

Whenever asked by my hairdresser or medical practitioner, "Are you comfortable?" I always respond with "I make a living, not a killing!"

Sandwiching "Old Betsy" between two spanking new hearses at the crematory loading bay, I wonder if my $695.00 direct cremation charge is less than what those families paid for their coaches alone!

Here are a few names that I have come across over the years etched on cemetery headstones: BURY, CHILL, CLOSE, COFFIN, CROAK, CURTAINS, GRAVES, GRIMM, MUMMY, PLANTEM, TAPS and one day,

AMEN.

Made in the USA
Middletown, DE
23 May 2021